COACHING FOR
EMOTIONAL
INTELLIGENCE

COACHING FOR
EMOTIONAL
INTELLIGENCE

The Secret to Developing the
Star Potential in Your Employees

Bob Wall

American Management Association

New York • Atlanta • Brussels • Chicago • Mexico City • San Francisco
Shanghai • Tokyo • Toronto • Washington, D.C.

Special discounts on bulk quantities of AMACOM books are available to corporations, professional associations, and other organizations. For details, contact Special Sales Department, AMACOM, a division of American Management Association, 1601 Broadway, New York, NY 10019.
Tel.: 212-903-8316.   Fax: 212-903-8083.
Web site: www.amacombooks.org

This publication is designed to provide accurate and authoritative information in regard to the subject matter covered. It is sold with the understanding that the publisher is not engaged in rendering legal, accounting, or other professional service. If legal advice or other expert assistance is required, the services of a competent professional person should be sought.

Library of Congress Cataloging-in-Publication Data

Wall, Bob (Bob Lee)
    Coaching for emotional intelligence : the secret to developing the star potential in your employees / Bob Wall.
        p.   cm.
    Includes bibliographical references and index.
    ISBN-10: 0-8144-0890-7
    ISBN-13: 978-0-8144-0890-2
    1. Employees–Coaching of.   2. Emotional intelligence–Study and teaching.
3. Performance–Psychological aspects.   4. Career development–Psychological aspects.   5. Management–Psychological aspects.   I. Title.

HF5549.5.C53W35 2007
658.3′124–dc22

                                                                                2006010834

Printing number

10   9   8   7   6   5   4

To my wife, Adrienne

CONTENTS

PART III

FROM THEORY TO PRACTICE: COACHING IN THE REAL WORLD   119

ACKNOWLEDGMENTS

I WANT TO EXPRESS MY GRATITUDE to Jack and Steve Simmons, developers of The Simmons Personal Profile and the EQ Profile. For thirty years, Simmons Management Systems has been dedicated to developing and perfecting an instrument that provides an uncannily accurate assessment of characteristics we now put under the heading of emotional intelligence. Their EQ Profile has proven to be invaluable in my work with clients in coaching for emotional intelligence. I am especially appreciative to Steve, Jill, and Bonnie for their gracious friendship and support.

To my friend and colleague, Wes Crane, my profound appreciation for his friendship and his mentorship in the interpretation of the EQ Profile. His insights into emotional intelligence have been a great influence in my development as a person and coach. His personal integrity and his generosity in sharing his time and knowledge have been an inspiration to me.

My thanks to my friend, Jerry Brooker, for his personal support and encouragement in helping me get into action and get this book written. He kept reminding me that books are written one day at a time and that my job was to make the best use of each of those days to make progress on the book. Thanks, Jerry, for helping me eat the elephant in small bites.

For the third time, my literary agent, John Willig of Literary

Services, Inc., has come through for me. His faith in my work and his relentless coaching in producing the best possible book proposal have once again produced results. Thanks, John, for your invaluable support.

My thanks to Adrienne Hickey, the editorial director at AMACOM Books, for her careful editing and for patiently helping me become a better writer. I also want to acknowledge Niels Buessem for his meticulous work in the final editing of the manuscript.

Finally, I owe a debt of gratitude to my wife, Adrienne. She understands that writing is an expression of my love for the work I get to do, and that creating a book consumes my time and mental energy. Without her patience and support, writing this book would not have been possible.

COACHING FOR
EMOTIONAL
INTELLIGENCE

INTRODUCTION

I WANT TO INVITE YOU to join me in a personal journey of self-exploration and discovery. This is a book about coaching people to develop their emotional intelligence. You cannot approach this topic as a coach without taking a close look at yourself and the life experiences, beliefs, attitudes, assumptions, and personal abilities that have shaped the development of your own emotional intelligence.

There is an underlying assumption present in all coaching: that the coach has developed deeper mastery of the knowledge and skills of a topic than the person receiving the coaching. For most managers, this is no problem when dealing with the technical aspects of the job. People get promoted and promoted again because they continue to demonstrate their insight into the knowledge, abilities, and skills necessary to perform well in their chosen professions.

We must bring the same assumption to coaching for emotional intelligence: that coaches have developed a higher level of mastery of emotional intelligence than the people they are coaching. This requires you to become a student of emotional intelligence and lead the way by embodying the characteristics you want to develop in others. This may strike you as an impossible standard to meet. In truth, it is.

The mastery of emotional intelligence is a life-long journey. As you set out to learn more about how to coach for emotional intelligence, it is important to bear three things in mind:

1. No one has perfect mastery of emotional intelligence. Each of us brings to this topic our own unique blend of strengths and characteristics that develop over a lifetime of experience.

2. As opposed to IQ that is fixed at birth, emotional intelligence is fluid and constantly evolving. As we grow older, our emotional intelligence continues to develop. Life experience shapes our perceptions of ourselves, our personal discipline and character, and how we deal with the interpersonal aspects of our lives.

3. This book contains Reflections, Skill Development, and Skill Application exercises. These are assignments designed to accelerate the growth and expression of your own emotional intelligence and your effectiveness as a coach. While the book is focused on coaching others, you cannot approach this topic without expanding your own self-awareness and developing greater mastery of those aspects of your emotional intelligence that present opportunities for growth.

Approach this book in the spirit of self-discovery. I've structured the writing much as I would structure conversations we would have if I were serving as your personal executive coach. Where appropriate, I will share some of the personal lessons that have been instrumental in my own development, not that I claim to be fully evolved emotionally. I don't know anyone who is. But the more we study this topic and apply what we learn to our own lives, the better we become at coaching others to develop their emotional intelligence.

AN OVERVIEW OF EXERCISES
INCLUDED IN THIS BOOK

If all you do is read this book, you might pick up some interesting information, but in the end, the time invested in your reading will make little or no difference in the quality of your coaching. This is not just another management book for you to read and put on the shelf. To gain the maximum benefit from the book, I am asking you to make a commitment to engage with this book in the same spirit you would if you had acquired an executive coach to develop your self-awareness and abilities as a leader. Executive coaches give people a variety of assignments to do in the course of their work with clients. In this book, I do much the same.

From time to time, I'll pose questions for you to consider, exercises to do, and skills to practice and incorporate into your leadership. All the "assignments" you'll find in the book are based on conversations and skill development sessions I've had working as an executive coach with my clients.

Executive coaching only works to the extent my clients invest themselves and their time in learning from the process. I'm counting on you to take time to reflect on the questions posed and do the exercises necessary to assist you in becoming a more effective coach. I know you are a busy person but the only way this book will make a difference for you is to make time available to follow directions where you find them.

This is not a race. Take time to do the exercises and the quality of your coaching will improve dramatically. You'll become more effective in offering praise. You'll become more at ease with corrective coaching when performance does not meet your standards. And the people you coach will show marked improvements in their performance. Pause right now and think about the people who report to you. What improvements in their performance would make it worth investing three to five hours in doing the assignments in this book?

I have worked very hard to make this an easy book to read: short, to the point, and including only the most essential information and theory. In most chapters, you will find assignments. These exercises have been carefully designed and sequenced to help you translate the concepts in the book into leadership skills you can put to use in your work. Three different kinds of assignments are presented:

1. *Reflections*

Coaching must produce changes in self-perception, knowledge, attitudes, and skills. In "Reflections," you will find questions or topics to consider. Learning new skills and actually using them on the job requires shifts in values, attitudes, and beliefs that will make you more willing to put new skills to work on the job. The Reflections have a very important purpose: for you to think about what you have been reading and translate it into your own experience.

A recommendation: You will gain so much more from this book if you invest time addressing each of the Reflections in writing. If you write, you will engage with the topics and questions more fully and state your opinions and feelings more clearly.

Like most leaders, you already have more than enough to do and you may not want to take the time to write about the Reflections. If I can't convince you to do the work in writing, at least take time to pause and reflect for a few moments on each of the questions and topics you'll find in the Reflections. Devoting a few minutes to each one is an important step in fully benefiting from this book.

2. *Skill Development*

Skill development requires mastering elements that, when put together properly, results in the development of a new skill. The coaching skills presented in this book have been under development from the time I first started leading workshops in the 1970s. These methods have been continuously refined to produce the greatest possible results with the least amount of effort required on your part. They are based on common sense and can be practiced, mastered, and easily put to use in the real world. The more time you devote to the exercises, the faster you'll feel comfortable putting these skills to use at work.

3. *Skill Applications*

This is the whole point of reading the book and doing the exercises: putting the skills to use at work and, with practice, developing skill mastery. As in learning any new skill, you might be awkward and self-conscious when trying these skills out for the first time. You'll have to think about each element of the skill and carefully put them to use as I've described them. You'll know you are developing skill mastery when using the skill requires less and less conscious attention and preparation.

The Reflections, Skill Development, and Skill Applications exercises can be used in the coaching you are doing with the people who report to you. The Reflections will lead to conversations that will help you better understand your employees and how to support their growth. If you are coaching people in leadership positions, they need to develop their coaching skills as well as their emotional intelligence. Before a coaching session, you will find it helpful to return to the book and review the Reflections, Skill Development, and Skill Applications exercises for ideas to bring to your coaching conversations.

A Word About Terminology

The coaching strategies in this book are appropriate for use by all levels of management. The subjects of coaching would differ for various levels of management but the principles of coaching apply just as well for a CEO as they do for a first-line supervisor. For simplicity of writing, I've chosen to use the terms "manager" and "leader" to refer to those proving the coaching, and the terms "associates," "employees," and "direct reports" in referring to those on the receiving end of the coaching.

PUTTING OUR CONVERSATION IN CONTEXT

You wouldn't hire executive coaches for your company without carefully looking into the background, training, experience, and qualities they bring to their work. Conversations with other executive coaches and organizational development specialists have revealed that we have discovered our passion for this kind of work by following very different pathways over the course of our careers. So I want to tell you just enough about myself to help you understand how I found my way into a career I love and the kinds of projects I do. Knowing my history will help you understand how I arrived at the coaching strategies you'll find in this book.

As I write these words, I've been an independent management consultant for 26 years. The purpose of my work is to accelerate leadership, team, and cultural development, creating more successful organizations while enhancing the quality of life for the people who work in them.

I am a clinical psychologist by training. As a graduate student working on a Ph.D., I participated in a federally funded project to provide interpersonal skills workshops for human service organizations. Little did I know that in joining this project, I was to find my life's calling. I discovered a passion for workshop design and group facilitation. Most of all, I came to love the challenge of studying complex human interactions and developing simple models and communication strategies to help people deal with these interactions more effectively.

I started experimenting with management training at a hospital where I was employed part time as a graduate student, and I found myself drawn to books on leadership and organizational development. I had completed all my course work and clinical training and had passed the comprehensive examination, qualifying me as a Ph.D. candidate, when the grant supporting our training project expired.

A small group of us from the project got together to discuss making a dramatic change in direction. We loved designing and leading workshops, so why not leave graduate school and move to the city of our choice to start a consulting and training business? We moved to Seattle in 1980, without a clue that trying to start a consulting business in a city where you don't know a soul was not a very good idea. But fortunately we didn't know what we didn't know.

For the first two or three years, if I was awake, I was working—designing and redesigning workshops, writing lectures, and designing strategies and skills to help people deal more effectively with the communication challenges they face at work. It was a period of tremendous creativity, hard work, and learning from clients about the challenges they faced at work every day.

Working with managers, we learned about the challenges of coaching and dealing with people who seemed to be committed to dancing to the beat of a different drummer. In stress management and conflict management workshops, we spent hours in discussions with hundreds of people learning about the problems people faced in their jobs and the difficulties they faced in their relationships with their managers and peers.

While I still do engagements as a stand-up trainer, my work is now almost completely devoted to organizational assessment, executive coaching, and helping leaders and teams get to where they want to go faster than they would get there on their own. I get involved in a wide variety of projects, including:

- I work with leaders who have recently taken the helm of a company or a division within a company. After they've cleaned house and developed a new direction, I assist them in rebuilding the trust, communications, culture, leadership, and teamwork necessary to get the organization moving as quickly as possible.

- I evaluate and coach leaders who are technically gifted but whose management styles are creating high turnover and low morale. The work involves determining whether these leaders can be saved and what it is going to take to make it happen.

- I help companies cope with growth, reorganization, and other forms of change.

- I work with individuals and teams whose relationships are fractured, affecting both productivity and morale.

- I work with organizations dealing with mergers and acquisitions, helping them recreate their cultural values and accelerate the development of newly forming teams.

The Organizational Snapshot

At the start of every consulting project, I do a series of private, confidential interviews with executives and managers as well as with a representative sampling of associates. The purpose of these interviews is to discover what life inside the company looks like from each person's point of view. What do they love about their jobs? What changes would they like to see made? What is working well? What isn't? What is going on beneath the surface? What problems are obvious to everyone but are not being addressed?

At the appropriate point in the interview, I ask about a list of executives and managers by name. I explain that, if I want to understand the culture and effectiveness of the organization, I need to know how people in management positions are doing. What do these people do well and what could they do differently that would make them more effective? Given the promise of complete anonymity, people are dying to talk about the source of most of their frustrations at work: management. I've learned about what managers do that drives people crazy, limiting the effectiveness of their teams and damaging morale. And I've also learned about great leaders and what makes them so inspiring at the organizational and personal level.

APPLYING LESSONS LEARNED
FROM MY CLIENTS

This book is based on the lessons I've learned in discussions about work with thousands of people in all walks of life and every level of their organizations. I've been privileged to work with people who trusted me enough to share their experiences with me in training rooms, corporate retreats, organizational development projects, and individual coaching sessions. They have allowed me to look into their lives and learn about life in their organizations and about work and the meaning it has in their lives. And I have also learned how important the relationships between leaders and their teams are in determining both the effectiveness of the teams and the satisfaction people find in doing their work.

Everything you find in this book is distilled from what I have learned from people much like you, discussing what leaders and their teams want and need from each other, and developing simple principles and communication strategies to help people create lives at work that are both productive and the source of deep satisfaction and meaning.

The coaching skills in these pages have been tested and refined based on feedback from my clients. If you incorporate these skills into your leadership activities, I promise that you will become more effective and more personally comfortable with the whole activity of coaching.

My approach to coaching is based on common sense: techniques that are easy to learn, remember, and apply in the pressured environment of work. You'll find that you already know much of what you will read in this book. We'll reorganize what you know and provide communication strategies that will lead to improved performance by your direct reports.

But simple does not necessarily mean easy. Any change in human behavior takes work and results in discomfort for a time. You'll be trying on new behaviors and may feel awkward and uncomfortable at first. But with practice, these skills will feel more natural and, in time, they will become integrated into your leadership style.

Coaching Doesn't Have to Be Hard

It strikes me that the topic of performance management has become overly complicated. Leaders get so caught up in creating performance agreements and complying with organizational requirements for performance management that the whole point of coaching has been lost. Coaching, as defined in this book, is nothing more complex than having conversations with employees about their performance. If conversations about performance are infrequent or nonexistent, no formal organizational rituals or paperwork can possibly result in anything that approximates responsible employee and leadership development.

Now let's get to work.

PART I

THE IMPACT OF EMOTIONAL INTELLIGENCE ON COACHING AND DEVELOPMENT

CHAPTER 1

UNDERSTANDING EMOTIONAL INTELLIGENCE

COACHING FOR EMOTIONAL INTELLIGENCE requires that we understand it and how it affects the success of individuals and organizations. Once we begin to study it, we cannot help but reflect on the development of our own emotional intelligence and the role it plays in our personal and professional lives.

As a coach, you cannot give away what you have not first developed in yourself. The study of emotional intelligence leads us to these questions:

- In what ways am I expressing emotional intelligence in my work and in my life?

- Where do I need further development and how would improvements in my emotional intelligence affect my life and my work?

THE EMERGENCE OF EMOTIONAL INTELLIGENCE: WHY SHEER BRAINPOWER JUST ISN'T ENOUGH

In the early study of intelligence and the development of measures of IQ, psychologists focused on cognitive skills, such as problem solving, pattern recognition, and memory. As instruments to measure intelligence were developed, it soon became clear that IQ tests were only measuring a limited subset of the abilities that are necessary to develop a full and successful life. When I administered IQ tests, I learned little about the person other than how fast they could do simple cognitive tasks. David Wechsler, the developer of the standard IQ Test still in use today, wrote that "I have tried to show that in addition to intellective there are also non-intellective factors that determine intelligent behavior."[1] In my graduate training in psychology in the 1970s, IQ scores were seen as important but limited in predictive value. About the only thing IQ seemed to predict was a person's ability to succeed in school.

In the 1980s, psychologists like Howard Gardner began to write seriously about "multiple intelligence." He proposed that "intrapersonal and interpersonal intelligences" were just as important to overall life success as the cognitive abilities being measured in standard IQ tests.[2] But it wasn't until 1990 that the term "emotional intelligence" was coined by two psychologists who defined it as "a form of social intelligence that involves the ability to monitor one's own and others' feelings and emotions to discriminate among them, and to use this information to guide one's thinking and action."[3]

DEFINING EMOTIONAL INTELLIGENCE

In the past fifteen years or so, much has been written about emotional intelligence. The emerging body of research demonstrates the powerful role it plays in the workplace and in our lives. Various experts in the field have offered definitions and models to help us better understand what emotional intelligence is and how it affects success in life and work.

I prefer the model of emotional intelligence developed in *The EQ Difference,* by Adele B. Lynn.[4] Her work, which includes a method of self-coaching to develop emotional intelligence, has had a profound effect on me. Reading her book in conjunction with this one is sure to pay off, both for you and for the people you are coaching.

LYNN'S MODEL OF EMOTIONAL INTELLIGENCE

The following components of emotional intelligence are drawn from Chapter 6 of Lynn's *The EQ Difference:*

1. *Self-Awareness and Self-Control:* The ability to fully understand oneself and to use that information to manage emotions productively.

2. *Empathy:* The ability to understand the perspectives of others.

3. *Social Expertness:* The ability to build genuine relationships and bonds and to express caring, concern, and conflict in healthy ways.

4. *Personal Influence:* The ability to positively lead and inspire others, as well as oneself.

5. *Mastery of Purpose and Vision:* The ability to bring authenticity to one's life by living a life based on deeply felt intentions and values.[5]

As you are about to see, I have taken some liberties in adapting Lynn's model for use in this book. I will begin with her fifth component, Mastery of Purpose and Vision, which I have relabeled, "Mission, Vision, and Guiding Principles." That discussion is followed by the other four components in order.

MASTERY OF MISSION, VISION, AND GUIDING PRINCIPLES

Years ago I led a retreat for a company in the Northwest. My client was a competitive sailor who owned his own sailboat. He offered to sail a group of us across Puget Sound to the convention center where I would be facilitating a team development and planning retreat. The winds that day were calm, so we motored across the Sound rather than using the sails.

After we had been underway for a while, he asked me if I would like to take the helm. I explained that I had grown up in the Midwest, had never been onboard a sailboat, and was clueless as to what to do. He pointed to a feature in the land across the Sound and said, "See that cluster of trees on that point over there? That is your steering point."

"My what?"

"Your steering point. Every time the pointy end of the boat—we call it the bow—veers away from those trees, just bring the bow back to those trees. Keep aiming at the steering point and we will end up where we want to go."

The "steering point" has ever since been the way I think about the roles that purpose, vision, and core values play in our own lives. We are going to examine each element of the steering point in turn.

While most companies have a statement of mission and values, these all too often remain words on paper that are not used as a powerful leadership tool. Some companies write statements that are too long to absorb in a meaningful way. Others write mission statements, hang a copy in the lobby area, and include them in their marketing materials, but they do little else to make the work "take" at a cultural level.

Individual work units, such as a division or a department, should have their own statement of mission and values that is marked by three characteristics:

1. The unit's statement should flow out of and be consistent with the company's mission, vision, and values.

2. It should be tailored to the unit, taking into consideration what the unit does and who is defined as the primary customer.

3. You, as the leader of the unit, should not write this statement on your own. If you get a representative group of no more than ten people to assist you in crafting the document and then sharing it with the rest of the team, you will build support for it that you cannot build if you had written it on your own. Once the document has been crafted, discussed by the team, and a final revision has been created, that document forms the foundation for your team's work, its culture, and for your activity as a coach. In the Skill Application exercise at the end of this chapter, you will find a plan that will enable you to lead your group through the creation of a document that is uniquely tailored to your group.

Defining the mission of your work should be fairly easy. In what ways does your work support the achievement of the mission of your company? All work, no matter what form it might take, provides a form of service that makes a difference in the world. This is true of all jobs, no matter how mundane and ordinary the job might seem to be.

As an example, during a leadership development session at a hospital, I was leading a discussion about ways in which leaders can remind people that all work serves a broader purpose. The head of the housekeeping department raised his hand and said, "The work my people do could be reduced to mopping floors and cleaning toilets. I want them to know that what we are really doing is building trust." Intrigued, I asked him to elaborate. "If a patient's family walks into the hospital and sees dirt in the corners of the room and bathrooms that are anything less than absolutely spotless and shining, they are going to have doubts about what kind of care their loved one is receiving here. I am always reminding my staff that what we do is a very important element of the trust we want patients and their families to have in this institution and the services we provide."

Your group's mission statement should be short, memorable, and inspire you and your team to go to work, knowing that your work has meaning and is making a difference in the world. Suppose you lead a payroll department. Your mission might read something like this: "We ensure the on-time and accurate delivery of paychecks so that every family in our company has the security of managing their budgets knowing that the money will there as expected 100 percent of the time."

When people speak of their purpose, integrity of purpose reveals itself in two ways. First, you look for the presence or absence of personal passion and commitment in discussing the work they do. In listening to the head of housekeeping mentioned above, you knew that his words were coming from his heart. He passed the "gut test." When people speak of values that don't come from the heart, you can almost always tell that their words carry little weight and meaning.

The most telling indication of integrity takes place over a longer period of time. Listen to what people say. Then watch what they do. Nothing creates cynicism more than empty proclamations from leaders whose behavior gives lie to their promises.

Vision

Given the strategic goals of your business and the current state of the group you lead, what changes should be made over the next three to five years that will enable your team to make the greatest contribution to your company's success? A team without vision is like a crew on a boat without a destination. Once your team's long-term vision has been defined, you then define short-term action plans to move in the direction of accomplishing your long-range vision.

Defining your own personal long-range vision is equally important. What do you personally want to accomplish in your career in the next five years? In what ways will you need to develop yourself as a leader and coach in order to realize your personal vision? What can you start doing *now* to make your vision a reality?

Without defining your personal vision, you are in danger of allowing life circumstances and unexpected events to take charge in steering your life. Some people's lives unfold without direction. They bounce from job to job, sometimes ending up doing something "temporarily" because they need to pay the bills. They may know that to realize their dreams, they need to go back to school for more training, but the next thing they know, babies and bills start absorbing their time and money. Unless people make a conscious decision to make things happen, they can end up in their 50s or 60s, looking back on life as a series of squandered opportunities to pursue their dreams.

Guiding Principles

In addition to establishing your team's purpose and vision, you must also articulate your team's guiding principles. These are the values that will guide you and your team in accomplishing your work. At the same time, they help create a culture of a productive and life-enhancing work environment for everyone involved.

SELF-AWARENESS AND SELF-CONTROL

Self-awareness and self-control is the keystone of emotional intelligence. Helping people develop greater self-awareness is the fundamental goal of coaching. This means helping people see and own their strengths as well as revealing blind spots in their self-perception. These are behaviors and personal characteristics that serve to limit their personal and interpersonal effectiveness. Typically, people do not see these defects in themselves, even though they are often painfully obvious to everyone who works with and for them.

Expanding self-awareness includes becoming more aware of our feelings and how they drive our behavior. We must also become more aware of the values, beliefs, and assumptions that shape our view of the world and our place in it. Many of these are formed early in life and are unquestioned but powerful influences in how we interpret events and the degree of choice we feel is available to us moment by moment.

The greater our degree of self-awareness, the more we can develop self-control. Feelings, values, beliefs, and assumptions are constantly at work, shaping our experience. As we become more self-aware, we can focus this internal energy more productively, much like a camera lens focuses diffuse light to make it useful when it reaches the film.

Self-control certainly includes recognizing and managing negative emotions. For example, becoming more aware of the internal cues that tell us we are about to lose our temper puts us in a position to decide how to handle these emotions appropriately. But self-control also means drawing on our positive values, beliefs, and emotions to serve as the driving force to accomplish things that are important to us in life.

EMPATHY

Empathy finds its origins in our inner world but leads to expression in our outer world. Empathy might best be defined as the capacity to understand how individuals and groups interpret the events affecting their lives and how their emotional reactions to these events color the meaning that these events have for them.

The Inner World of Empathy

To develop empathy, we must care about the experiences, feelings, needs, and wants of the people around us. We must care enough to turn away from our self-centered thinking and focus on others to develop an understanding of the meaning and feelings associated with events occurring in their lives.

People who are completely lacking in empathy make terrible leaders. In fact, any role that requires developing relationships with people and understanding their needs suffers when empathy is lacking. Having the desire and ability to tune into others and understand the world from their point of view is one of the fundamental requirements for relationship-building. While empathy can be taught as a communication skill, if the inner quality of truly caring about other people and their feelings, needs, and wants is missing, training in the communication skills of empathy will do little good.

Do you have empathy? Another way of asking this question is, are you inner focused or outer focused? Do you spend most of your time thinking about your own concerns, plans, and worries to the extent that you rarely if ever give the other people in your life much thought? The irony of asking this question is that self-centered people rarely recognize how self-centered they are. The world revolves around them so it would never occur to them to think about the feelings and experience of other people.

In your conversations, what percentage of the conversation is spent talking about you versus what is going on with the other person? Generally, people who lack empathy don't ask much about other people. They don't care. It doesn't even occur to them to ask.

My wife has multiple sclerosis. In the years that I've known her, I've been struck by the two extremes I've seen in her relationships. There are people who always ask how she is doing and what they can do to help. Then they listen and let her talk about what is going on with her health and how it is affecting her.

Then there are those "friends" who can talk for an hour about the latest drama in their lives—who has done wrong to whom and how much that has inconvenienced them—but never once ask a question about how my wife has been feeling lately. Some people ask but don't wait to listen to the answer because they are off on the next event in their lives that compels them to describe it . . . in great detail.

Empathy is an essential working and leadership capacity. If you are going to build strong relationships with your direct reports, peers, bosses, customers, and vendors, you must have the capacity to understand what other people are feeling and wanting. Business is replete with two-way transactions. In order to close a sale, you must understand your customer's needs. If you are leading people through a difficult change, you must understand how the change is affecting them if you are going to be able to lead them effectively.

I once witnessed a great example of the value of empathy. I was working with the chief information officer of a company with an aggressive growth strategy that had resulted in the purchase of other companies. My client's job was to drive the migration of all the acquired company's data into his company's information systems, at which point the people in the acquired company would no longer have jobs. Yet he needed their cooperation and knowledge of their own systems to achieve a successful migration of data within the allotted time frame.

With each acquisition, he would call the acquired and about-to-disappear information systems group together. In his opening remarks, he would address the group and say something like this: "I know that this is a very difficult time for all of you. Many of you have worked together for years, and this acquisition means far more than just the loss of your positions. It means the loss of friendships that you have developed with each other as you experienced good times and difficult challenges working closely together. I know that you have families to take care of and bills to pay. I know how heavily that must be weighing on your minds at a time like this.

"I can't possibly accomplish the successful migration of the data to the home office without your assistance and cooperation. I want to make you a promise. I want to invite you to join me in a migration project that has as its theme, 'Nobody misses a paycheck.' You work hard with me to achieve a successful migration and I will make sure that our company does everything we can to support you in acquiring new positions in such a way that no one will miss a paycheck. In addition to a severance package, we will be providing outplacement support and, based on your performance during the migration, I'll be writing the best possible letters of recommendation I can. If we work hard together, we can pull this migration project off in such a way that everybody comes out of it a winner. We'll accomplish the migration on time and I will personally see to it that my company gives you the support you need to find a new position so that you don't have to worry about taking care of your families."

While the words he spoke were important, he delivered his message with such warmth, caring, and compassion for these people that he was able to build strong support for the migration of data and retain the people who were vital to the effort long enough to get the mission accomplished. By conveying his understanding of what these people were feeling in a warm and caring way, he built an amazing level of cooperation from the very people who were being asked to assist in engineering the disappearance of their jobs.

Empathy as a Communication Skill

Empathy is the fundamental relationship-building skill for establishing rapport. It is not enough to say, *"Yes. I understand what you are saying."* How many times have you heard someone say that when you knew he didn't have a clue what you were feeling or wanting to make happen at the time?

Developing empathy requires you to pay close attention to *what* people say and *how* they say it. Listen carefully to the words they use and pay close attention to other clues that convey what people are feeling and thinking, such as facial expressions, vocal tone and volume, pace of speech, gestures, and posture. Words alone convey only a small part of the totality of communication that tells us about another person's experience.

Empathy is an internal ability to resonate with another person's feelings, needs, and wants. Empathy is also a communication skill that can be practiced and developed. To use this skill in conversation, you have to pay close attention to what another person is saying and then put your understanding of the other person's experience into your own words. When you do this, one of two things will happen. When you are correct in your understanding and put it into your own words, this almost magically encourages people to keep talking and further explore the topic being discussed. If you are inaccurate in your perception, the other person will have the chance to clarify what she meant and help you avoid drawing inaccurate conclusions based on your misunderstanding of what she was saying.

As a communication skill, empathy serves two very important purposes. First, it is a way to test the accuracy of your listening. This is very important when speaking to your direct reports. When they know you understand them, it helps them feel closer to you. And if you don't understand them, if you don't put your understanding into your own words, they won't have the opportunity to clarify what they have been saying. Both of you will leave the conversations with misunderstandings of what just took place. When you are talking with customers, you want to make certain you understand what they are saying, how they feel about the topic being discussed, and what it means to them. Understanding is the pathway to customer service.

Beyond serving as an accuracy test for your listening, empathy serves another role that is even more important. Responding empathically to people shows that you care about them and that you are genuinely interested in listening to what they have to say. Empathic responding draws people out and encourages them to share their internal experience because they know that you are doing your best to make sure you understand what meaning the topic has for them.

Empathy builds the foundation for relationships with friends, direct reports, customers, and other people you encounter at work. People are far more open to being influenced when they know that you are actively involved in listening to them with the intention to understand their experience and how it is influenced by their feelings, needs, and wants.

SOCIAL EXPERTNESS

While empathy is a key ingredient of social expertness, building relationships takes other characteristics and skills as well. First, you must truly care about other people and have their best interests at heart. One man who stood out as a leader with the gift of knowing how to connect with people was the late Don Nakata. Don was the president and CEO of a family-owned chain of grocery stores in the Northwest.

Don was a living demonstration that loving people is an inspiring and effective form of leadership. Don was always visiting his stores and talking with the people who served his customers. In conversations, he had the capacity to make each person feel important and as the total focus of his attention. He would ask about their personal lives and go out of his way to ensure that people were able to take care of family needs. He freely shared his love of his business, providing food in stores that offered friendly and helpful service to all his customers.

He would always share the latest ideas he'd been thinking about and pass books along for people to read. Every conversation with Don allowed you to bathe in his warmth, his attention, his love of people and the grocery business, and his interest in you as a human being. And his people responded to his attention by sharing his values and providing warm and friendly services to their customers. When Don died, I knew the world had lost a man who had the rare ability to connect to people in a loving way that made his business successful while enriching the lives of everyone who came in contact with him. Whenever I hear people argue that you can't be close to people and manage them, I think of Don. Genuine warmth and love, freely expressed, can bring out the best in people.

In addition to caring about people and investing in their success, there are many other skills and personal qualities that contribute to social expertness. Some of these are quite subtle. For example, how do you carry yourself? Do you present yourself as an attractive, likeable person? Do you smile, make eye contact, and greet people with warmth and friendliness? Or do you wear your worries on your sleeve? Do you look distracted and absorbed by the problems and projects that are on your mind? Do you avoid eye contact and fail to greet people you meet in the halls and at meetings? Are you noticeably friendly to upper management but cold and distant to those lower down the corporate ladder than yourself?

Everything you do sends messages about you. Some of these messages produce unintended consequences. I've had some painful lessons to learn about this myself. I have what my wife calls a "down mouth." That is, when my face is relaxed, the corners of my mouth point down and make me look like I am frowning. For many years, I didn't smile very much because I was self-conscious about a couple of crooked teeth. My teeth had also been discolored by a medication taken in early childhood. My habit of not smiling only added to my tendency to appear overly serious and remote.

A friend of mine who used to coach actors suggested that I get my front teeth capped. When the dental work was complete, he asked me in to stand in front of a mirror and just relax my face and look at myself. Whether he was correct or not, he believed that men rarely look at themselves in the mirror. We get up in the morning, shave, and comb our hair and that is about it for mirror time. And when we are doing those tasks, we focus on getting a clean shave and getting rid of our "pillow hair." We aren't really looking at the image we take out into the world. He believed that men aren't aware of how their facial expressions appear to others. The only way to find out is to study your face in the mirror.

So I stood in front of a mirror, let my face relax, and looked at myself more closely than I ever had before. Given my "down mouth" and my habit of not smiling, I had to admit that my face projected a somber image of distance and self-absorption. I certainly wasn't projecting an image of outward friendliness or approachability. Given what I do for a living, this was a stunning and disturbing realization.

The next step was to practice something I can only describe as "lifting" the musculature of my face. That simple exercise produces a dramatic change in the message being sent by my facial expression. It makes me look softer, friendlier, and more approachable. I was then to practice adding a smile to the lifting of the facial muscles. What a difference this simple exercise has made. A friend of mine who is a therapist says that this exercise releases hormones that actually make us feel on the inside the way we want to appear on the outside.

I was told to keep practicing this exercise over and over again so that I would become more familiar with the difference in how these two expressions feel. Otherwise, it is too easy to slip back into a somber and unapproachable facial expression. I still do this exercise. I've found that, given the structure of my face, I have to do what feels like an exaggerated lifting and smiling to project an image of friendliness, openness, and approachability. Only then do I project the outer image of approachability that I am striving for. And, interestingly enough, when I make my outer appearance project that image, I feel softer and happier on the inside.

This exercise may sound silly to you but try it yourself. You can, after all, lock the bathroom door and do this exercise without anyone observing you and wondering what in the world you are doing. You might be surprised by what you discover about the messages your face is sending and how a simple lifting of your face and a smile produces real results, inside and out.

There are so many behaviors that play a role in social expertness. You must constantly remind yourself that you want to be perceived as an approachable and likeable person. One element means *looking* approachable and likable. But other behaviors play a role. Here are just a few to consider:

• Reach out to people you don't know in a meeting and introduce yourself, with a smile on your face.

• Ask questions about the other people and show a genuine interest in what they have to say. If small talk is hard for you, ask people where they grew up and how they happened to get into their profession. What do they like about their work? What challenges are they facing in their department? What are they doing about them? In a more social setting, you can ask people what they like to do for relaxation. Or you can ask them about current events or politics.

• It helps to remember that many other people are just as uncomfortable as you are and are just waiting for someone to break the ice and start a conversation. These conversations are good opportunities to practice your empathy skills. Listen carefully to what other people are saying and how they say it. What does that tell you about the meaning the topic has for them and how they feel about it? Then use your own words to paraphrase what you think the person has said. If you are right, it will draw them out to say more. If you are a bit off the mark, then they'll clarify what they said so that you can develop a correct understanding of them.

• You may also have some habits to break. Do you use sarcastic humor? Do you have a tendency to interrupt people? Are the expressions on your face intimidating and likely to shut people down? Do you dominate meetings and don't give others space to express themselves? Do you come across as cold and distant? Think about people you have known over your career and you can add many other behaviors to the list that undermine social expertness.

- Shyness or long-established personal reserve may be something you must work on to expand your personal effectiveness. One way to do this is to ask yourself this question: What would I look like if I weren't shy? How would I carry myself? How would I behave around people? Get as clear a picture in your mind of this as possible. Then simply start acting that way. There are two routes to changing certain psychological traits. One is to pursue years of therapy, in hopes that working on your feelings will lead to a change in behavior.

There is another option that will produce faster results. With a clear picture in mind of how you want to behave, start acting that way, even though it takes you out of your comfort zone. Force yourself to start acting in a more outgoing way. The more you do this, the more comfortable you will feel with the new behaviors. Introverts actually can learn to behave more like extroverts. It just takes time, practice, and the personal courage necessary to try on new behaviors. You can expect to feel uncomfortable at first, but in time you can develop a more outgoing way of interacting with people. Remember that it is all but impossible to establish personal influence if you hide your light under a basket.

The challenge of developing social expertness is that we can be blind to our own behaviors and may unintentionally do things that create social distance from people at work. Many companies use various forms of 360-degree feedback instruments to provide feedback to people about how they are perceived by their peers, direct reports, and managers. But many of these instruments fail to provide the detail necessary to help you understand exactly what you are doing that puts people off and how to go about making the necessary adjustments in your behavior.

Want to know more about how people perceive you? Or would you like to gather more specific feedback on something in your 360-degree assessment report? The best way is to ask for direct feedback from people who know you reasonably well and have the strength of character to be honest with you. But this can be an awkward conversation, especially for those who report to you. In my book, *Working Relationships,* you will find a method for structuring these kinds of conversations.[6]

PERSONAL INFLUENCE

You may have already noticed that the elements of Adele Lynn's model of emotional intelligence build on each other. First, self-awareness and self-control. Then empathy, the ability to connect with and understand the experience and feelings of other people at work, both as individuals and as groups. Next, social expertness. Simply stated, this refers to a wide array of personal characteristics and communication skills that allow you to establish a connectedness with others. Being seen as an attractive and credible person opens the door to establishing personal influence.

Building on all these elements, you will develop the personal influence required to make things happen with and through other people in a positive way. Certainly, some people get their way by being domineering and aggressive, but this kind of influence is likely to fail over the long haul.

I've observed many people who have developed powerful influence in their organizations. They all have several things in common:

- *Technical Mastery.* No matter how skilled you might be socially, it won't get you very far if you don't know what you are talking about. Developing influence requires the dedication to be constantly learning and expanding your base of knowledge in your chosen field.

- *Interpersonal Connectedness.* If you want to develop influence, you must consciously work on developing relationships throughout the organization, drawing on the first three capacities in Lynn's model of emotional intelligence. Your level of personal influence is a combination of your technical credibility and the network of relationships you have built in your organization. People need to trust that you know what you are doing professionally and they must see you as a likeable and trustworthy person.

• *Careful Timing of Emotional Expression and Emotional Control.* It is impossible to leave our emotions at the door when we go to work in the morning. Emotionally intelligent leaders know how to control their emotions and how to express them appropriately. When I react emotionally without thinking, I sometimes say something that makes me wish that, with a sharp intake of breath, I could suck the words right back into my mouth. Lack of emotional control can do substantial damage to our credibility and relationships. The free and undisciplined expression of anger can be a career-limiting activity for someone in a line position. Lack of emotional control in a leader can create an atmosphere of fear and intimidation that affects productivity, the expression of ideas, and the morale for those reporting to that manager.

The expression of emotion plays an important role in leadership. Great leaders inspire others by sharing freely what inspires and excites them in a way that invites others to join them in the pursuit of a particular goal or expression of a value. Expressing pride and gratitude for work well done motivates people to work even harder to accomplish those kinds of results in the future. Anger, appropriately phrased and expressed, can catalyze a team into action in a time of crisis caused by poor performance.

• *The Ability to Convince, Persuade, and Inspire.* Great ideas go nowhere unless they are shared in a way that inspires and invites others to turn the ideas into action. The most persuasive people do this in a way that can best be described as selfless. Their intentions are clearly focused on what is best for the company and the customers it serves.

• *The Ability to Deal with Conflict Professionally.* Conflict is inevitable at work. One of the essential abilities of developing influence is the capacity to deal with difficult issues without taking things personally. Persuasion lies in managing those emotions that can derail a conversation and in keeping discussion focused on what is good for the company and its customers. My book, *Working Relationships,* deals with how conflicts get taken personally and offers simple methods for "professionalizing" conflict rather than "personalizing" it.

Skill Application: Creating Statements of Mission, Vision, and Guiding Principles

The following work is best accomplished by a group of no more than ten people who are representative of your entire group. If you lead a large division, you will share the work with the rest of the group for their reactions before finalizing the document. Just follow each step as described and you will find that you can create your unit's mission statement, vision, and values and end up with a product you can be proud of in a much shorter period of time than you might ever thought possible.

Materials required: Two easel stands and several 3M Sticky Note Easel Pads (like the Sticky Notes on your desk but the size of an easel pad. This allows you to easily post the work you and your group will be doing without using tape or thumbtacks.) You will also need a supply of permanent markers. (Don't use the kind made for erasable white boards. They quickly evaporate and produce fainter and fainter markings.) Ask the participants to bring clipboards, writing paper, and pens.

Step 1. Create Your Unit's Mission Statement
Have two easel stands in the front of the room, equipped with the 3M Pads. Draw a horizontal line through the center of each pad, dividing each page into two equal halves.

Then address the group, explaining that you are about to work together to create your unit's mission statement. In writing a mission statement, you must discuss four topics, each of which you use to label the four sections you've created on the two easel pads:

1. Who are we?
2. What do we do?
3. For whom do we do it?
4. Why is our work important?

Now lead a discussion of each item, recording short "bullets" to capture the major topics of the discussion. As the facilitator of this exercise, encourage open discussion without making any judgments at this stage. While the written product ultimately created is important, the discussions leading up to its creation are as important as the writing itself.

Any comment is fair game and should be listed, with one exception. Profit, shareholder value, and other financial measures should not be included in defining your group's mission statement. If and when it comes up, say something like, "Yes, it is important to increase shareholder value. But we will do that when we are accomplishing our mission. Profit is a yardstick that tells us whether or not we are getting our job done."

Remember that what you ultimately want to craft is a statement of mission or purpose that touches the heart and defines the ultimate meaning of the work you do. That you have to make a profit is a given. If you don't, your company won't be around long to make its unique contribution to making a better world. You want your unit's mission statement to appeal to that part in most of us that wants to know that what we do is important, meaningful, and inspiring. While "shareholder value" is a critical business measure, it is not particularly exciting to get out of bed in the morning to go make money for your stockholders or private owners. Meaning and inspiration come from how we define the work itself.

Here are some experiences you might run into in the discussion:

- *Who are we?* This is usually fairly easily defined. People might just use the name of your division. But sometimes the discussion goes in a broader direction, especially if people in the group have divergent opinions about how they define the group for themselves. If this happens, that is great. Just keep listing bullets and encouraging the expression of differing points of view.

- *What do we do?* This should result in a quick listing of a variety of activities, products, and services provided by the group. No judgments. Just keep listing.

- *For whom do we do it?* When I lead this exercise, I am sometimes surprised to find that a group lacks a shared understanding of who their customer actually is. This can lead to a rich discussion. Is your group's customer another department within the organization? Your company's employees? Or do they see the customer as defined by the ultimate purchaser of your company's products and services? Encourage discussion of differing points of view and list bullets to capture the various opinions present in the group.

- *Why is our work important?* In introducing this section of the discussion, ask your group to focus on what makes your team's work meaningful. In what ways are they making a difference in the lives of your customers? How does their work contribute to make the world a better place? Encourage the group to speak from the heart. You are looking for lofty statements of why your work is important.

Circle words and phrases that stand out to the group. Once you've discussed all four questions, ask the group to look at the bullets and phrases and identify those that stand out as particularly on point. Carefully circle each one identified so that the wording is still legible.

Ask each individual to write a mission statement. Each person writes a mission statement, drawing from the work done on the easel pads. Stick an easel pad paper on the wall or on a third easel in the front of the room. Write the words, "Short, memorable, and inspiring." Make a comment that mission statements should be short and easily committed to memory. The wording of the statement should be inspiring and heartfelt.

Then write on the pad the words, "Capture the purpose and meaning of our work." Note that the mission statement does not have to even draw on phrases from all four questions. Just ask each person to write a short mission statement that captures, in their words, the conversation they've had up to now about the mission of the team.

Ask people to pair up. Once each person has written a mission statement, ask them to pair up, compare their statements, and collapse them into a single mission statement that captures the best elements of each one's writing. Give them two sheets of easel pad paper (one thickness of paper sometimes ends up with permanent marker ink bleeding through and marking the wall) and ask them to record their combined mission statement on the paper in large block letters.

If you have ten people, you will now have five versions of mission statements. Post them together on one wall and ask people to come up and review them. In a discussion, circle the best words and phrases from each statement.

Now work with a blank easel pad in the front of the room and, as a group, write one version of your mission statement, drawing from the circled words and phrases in the five statements on the wall. You may end up with a version that has several different phrases or words that are included to be considered in the final statement. Then work with the group on revising the statement to craft a final draft that captures the group's thinking. You'll know you are close when people start to get excited about the phrasing that is emerging in the discussion.

Sometimes, someone in the group will turn out to be a good wordsmith and put together a statement that captures the agreement of the entire group. Again, as long as it produces an emotional response of excitement and agreement, you've gotten the job done.

Let the work "soak" for a few days. You can continue with the next steps but sometimes it is a good idea to break and meet again in a few days. If you do so, save all easel pad papers so that you can repost everything on the wall. This kind of work is taxing for some people, depending on your profession. I've seen groups excited but clearly ready to stop at this point. Then when they reconvene, some people may have a fresher perspective on the writing, resulting in editing that makes your mission statement a much better piece of writing.

Step 2. Create a Glossary of Terms

Once the mission statement wording is complete, ask for a group of three or four people to meet at another time and create a *Glossary of Terms*. You have worked hard on writing a short, pithy statement. Now use the Glossary to further define key words and phrases. Because this document will be used to communicate, make sure that each word and phrase is carefully chosen. Suppose you are bringing a new hire into the team. You would share the mission statement with her and then give her the Glossary, which further defines what the team means by "world-class service," "the end user," or "enhances the quality of life."

Step 3. Create a Long-Range Vision and Short-Term Goals

Introduce this topic by reviewing the company's strategic goals. Lead a discussion of the state of your division or department today and, given where the company wants to go in the future, what your department should look like in three to five years.

List bullets and ideas. This should be a wide-ranging conversation, all focusing on what your group must accomplish in the next three to five years to make a contribution to the realization of your company's strategy for the future. This can include anything from the use of new technologies to the development of new products and services. Anything is fair game for this discussion.

Then ask for two or three volunteers to use the ideas to create a narrative description of your team's vision—no longer than two to three short paragraphs in length. Ask them to produce a document that describes, in inspirational wording, the team's vision for its future. Adjourn to give the volunteers time to complete this written document. Before reconvening the group to continue its work, review the document to make certain the vision statement is consistent with your own plans for the development of your department.

Upon reconvening, distribute copies of the vision statement to the group. After allowing time for a discussion of the vision statement, work with the group to create three to five goals that, if achieved, would enable the team to realize its vision.

Then, for each goal, create an action plan to be implemented over the next 12 to 18 months to move in the direction of realizing your vision.

Step 4. Establish Your Group's Guiding Principles

Now create five to seven Guiding Principles for each of the following three topics: the work itself, culture and teamwork, and leadership. Discuss each topic in the following order:

1. Our Guiding Principles for the Work Itself. In order to live up to your mission statement and accomplish your long-range vision, what values need to guide every person in the group as they go about doing their work?

These guiding principles will vary depending on the kind of work you do. For example, in a hospital, one principle might read, "We treat each of our patients as if they were members of our own family." In a manufacturing facility, a principle might read, "Close is never good enough. We strive for perfection in every product we make." In a retail business, a principle might read, "We live by the 10-3 rule. We smile within 10 feet of a customer. We greet customers within 3 feet, by name if possible."

When you have listed five to seven principles relating to the work itself, move on to the next topic. Restrict each list to no more than seven. This forces the group to list the most important values for each step of the discussion.

2. Our Guiding Principles for Our Culture and Teamwork. Every company has a culture, either the one that evolves on its own or the one the group consciously creates. This is your opportunity to lead the group in creating a culture based on emotional intelligence. Come to this session prepared to introduce the topic of emotional intelligence, drawing on the discussion of Lynn's model discussed earlier in this chapter. After introducing the five components of emotional intelligence, ask the group to list behaviors or competencies associated with each component. Using an easel pad, list the group's ideas for each of the five stages.

Then lead them in creating guiding principles that will enable the team to create a culture that has two goals in mind: one, getting the job done while two, creating a great place to work. Ask the group this question: What values would support us, individually and as a group, in being as productive and efficient as possible and also create a satisfying and rich working experience for every member of the team?

You may end up with guiding principles such as:

"We welcome and encourage the expression of ideas to find better ways of getting things done."

"We keep our promises . . . to ourselves, to each other, and to our customers."

"We acknowledge each other for work well done."

3. Our Guiding Principles for Our Leadership. Everything written up to this point will only be accomplished if every leader—from you as the unit's head manager to first-line supervisors—behaves in ways that support the creation of a culture that is both productive and enriching to the lives of everyone on the team. Again, referring to the principles of emotional intelligence, lead the group in creating those guiding principles that would produce the qualities of leadership necessary to support the creation of the ideal working environment. These principles might include the following:

"Every leader is open to disagreement and encourages the expression of diverse opinions."

"Our leaders hold themselves accountable for the productivity and well-being of the people they lead."

"Leaders promise to praise or acknowledge their team members at least once every week."

Make sure that your planning group includes nonmanagers as well as managers. Having this mixed group develop your leadership's guiding principles enables representatives of your line staff to describe what qualities they'd like to see embodied in their leadership. This adds the weight to groups' expectations that your leadership team "walk the talk" in their future leadership practices. It also empowers you, as the team's leader, to hold the group's managers and supervisors accountable for living up to the values described in these guiding principles. Share the written product with every member of the team. Once the product is complete, hold a series of meetings in which team members get a chance to react to each segment of the writing. You may end up refining the wording of certain parts of the document if the discussions indicate the need.

The overriding goal of these discussions is to get buy-in from every member of the team. Giving them the chance to discuss the *guiding principles*, for example, creates ownership of these values and a commitment to live up to them. Also ask questions like,

"Where are there gaps that need to be closed? This is a statement of our ideals and there will always be ways in which we can do a better job of living up to these ideals." Work with each team in your division or department, identifying gaps between where they are today and where they want to be. Create action plans to address gaps as needed.

Constantly look for opportunities to tie your coaching to your mission, vision, and guiding principles. This written document becomes one of the major topics of coaching conversations. For example, if you see someone doing something that is consistent with one of your values for the work itself or the culture, you have the opportunity to praise someone and underline that importance of that value. On the other hand, performance or behavior that undermines your mission statement or is inconsistent with your guiding principles is the opportunity to offer corrective feedback.

One of the key elements of emotional intelligence is the mastery of vision and purpose. Your vision and purpose is made real only to the extent that you share it and bring it up in the course of doing your work every day. Bring this principle to your coaching activities: You get what you talk about. In making decisions or coaching your staff, make reference to your company's mission and values as an essential part of your communication. This reinforces the importance of these statements and that they are not just words on paper.

One final test of the meaning of this work is whether you have a leader on your team who is clearly out of step with your mission, vision, and guiding principles. If so, are you taking action to either correct their performance or remove them from their position? Nothing creates cynicism faster than allowing leaders to remain in their positions who are clearly out of step with what you have proclaimed to be important to the success and vitality of your team.

Reflections

The following "assignments," which will take an hour or so to complete, are the longest assignments you will find in the entire book. They are also among the most important. Again, I want to encourage you to do these Reflections in writing. They build the foundation for the work you'll be doing in the remainder of the book.

Reflections: Self-Awareness and Self-Control

1. How well do you manage your emotions at work? Of the entire range of emotions, which emotions do you express in ways that benefit your effectiveness? Which emotions do the greatest damage to your effectiveness and your relationships? What do you need to do to stop doing damage to yourself and others regarding the expression of these emotions?

2. Do you treat your direct reports any differently from how you treat your peers or superiors? If so, in what ways? Why do you treat your direct reports differently from others in the organization? What message is this sending about how you value them and feel about them? What message is this sending about the kind of person you are?

3. Are you willing to ask people for feedback to uncover blind spots, that is, behaviors that unintentionally have a negative effect on your relationships at work? If not, what are you afraid that you might learn about yourself?

Reflections: Empathy

1. Take time to reflect on how each of your associates is doing, both at work and in their lives. Do you ask enough questions and listen carefully enough to know how they are doing? Are you aware of the personal challenges faced in life by your associates?

Do you support them in meeting their personal challenges? Even listening and allowing them to talk is a form of emotional support. And emotional support makes people more productive at work when they are facing challenges in their personal lives.

2. Are you able to describe the professional aspirations of each of your direct reports? If not, ask about them.

3. Do you make a conscious effort to listen and respond to the emotional needs of your staff?

4. Are you able to read the emotions of a group and frame your communications to take their emotions into account and make them more receptive to your message?

5. Do you believe that responding to the emotions of people at work is either inappropriate or unnecessary and outside the boundaries of a professional relationship?

- If so, what experiences led to the formulation of this belief?
- Is staying emotionally detached from your staff a way to avoid having to deal with some of the complexities of relationships at work?
- While there might be some gains adopting this strategy, what are the negative consequences of emotional detachment?
- How does detachment affect your relationships with your staff and their willingness to be open with you?

Reflections: Social Expertness

1. Rate your ability to build relationships at work on a scale of 1 to 10. To the degree that you rated yourself anything less than a 10, in what ways do you need to make improvements in your ability to build relationships?

2. Make a list of all the people who are important to you in accomplishing your work and the work of your team. Rate each relationship on a scale of 1 to 10. What do you need to do differently to improve the quality of each of these relationships?

3. Do you have any social habits or skills that need to be improved to make you more effective at work? What are you doing about it? (Adele Lynn's *The EQ Difference* provides excellent suggestions for self-observation to become more aware of yourself and messages you may be sending unintentionally.)[7]

4. How well do you know your direct reports and your peers? Do you know the names of their spouses and children? Do you know about any personal challenges they face in their lives, such as a chronic illness in the family? Do you know what they like to do for relaxation? Do they have hidden talents and passions you are unaware of, such as painting, ballroom dancing, or volunteer work in the community?

Reflections: Personal Influence

1. On a scale of 1 to 10, rate your ability to influence the thinking and decisions made by other people at work. What improvements do you need to make to establish greater influence? Do you need to work on building more relationships? Do you need to become a more articulate advocate of your ideas? Do you hold back out of fear of rejection or looking bad? What are you doing about the need to make any improvements? Make a plan of action and act on it.

2. Imagine your staff were to gather somewhere after work one night and have a conversation about you. What would you like them to say about the kind of person you are as a boss? What do you fear they might say about you?

3. In giving directions to your staff, do you give commands or do you frame your directions so people understand the purpose of what they are being asked to do and how their efforts will contribute to the company and the customers you serve? Look for opportunities to refer to your company's mission and values in explaining decisions or giving directions.

4. Do people like to work for you? If not, what is missing in your relationships with them that would make their work more meaningful and enjoyable? Do you believe that people need to do what they are told and that whether or not they feel connected to you and enjoy their work is not your problem? If you feel that way, take an honest look at whether or not you are willing to make some changes in your leadership style.

NOTES

1. D. Wechsler, "Nonintellective Factors in General Intelligence," *Psychological Bulletin* 37 (1940): 444–445.

2. H. Gardner, *Frames of Mind* (New York: Bantam Books, 1983).

3. P. Salovey and J. D. Mayer, "Emotional Intelligence," *Imagination, Cognition and Personality* 9, 3 (1990): 185–211.

4. Adele B. Lynn, *The EQ Difference* (New York: AMACOM, 2005). www.amacombooks.org. Excerpted by permission of the publisher.

5. Ibid., pp. 39–40.

6. Bob Wall, *Working Relationships* (Palo Alto, Calif.: Davies-Black Publishing, 1999), pp. 153–159.

7. Lynn, *The EQ Difference,* Chapter 8, Step 1: Observe, pp. 50–78.

CHAPTER 2

THE ROLE OF EMOTIONAL INTELLIGENCE IN PROFESSIONAL SUCCESS

THE SCIENTIFIC STUDY of emotional intelligence has only begun to scratch the surface of this fascinating topic. Yet there is already ample evidence that it plays a huge role in success on the job, especially in professions that require high intelligence, engage people in complex work, or bring people into frequent contact with others in doing their work.

EMOTIONAL INTELLIGENCE AND THE COMPLEXITY OF WORK

In jobs of medium complexity, such as clerical workers and mechanics, top performers are 12 times more productive than those at the bottom and 85 percent more productive than the average performer. In jobs that are more complex, such as insurance sales and the management of financial accounts, top performers are 127 percent more productive than those whose performance was judged to be average.[1]

The interesting question is: What accounts for the difference between star performers and average performers? Presumably, people in these jobs have roughly the same training and experience. In competency research in over 200 companies worldwide, Daniel Goleman found that the differences in performance can best be understood as a function of differences in emotional intelligence. Technical skills and IQ accounted for only one third of variance in performance. The remaining two thirds of the variance was accounted for by emotional intelligence.[2]

L'Oreal decided to start hiring salespeople based on certain aspects of emotional intelligence and compared how they performed relative to people selected the old way. Looking at performance over a period of a year, individuals chosen for emotional intelligence generated $91,370 more than those chosen the old way. This resulted in a net revenue increase of $2,558,360! The new group of salespeople also yielded 63 percent less turnover in the first year as compared to the salespeople chosen the traditional way.[3]

In this one study selecting people for emotional intelligence generated a dramatic increase in sales as well as a huge savings by reducing turnover. Turnover is costly. First, a pool of people must be interviewed, hired, and trained. Then they must remain on the job long enough for the company to identify those who are not suited for the work. These people then have to be separated from the company, and the screening of applicants starts all over again. And all the time these people were in their positions they were underperforming, generating lower sales, adding yet another financial drain on the company's resources.

The United States Air Force recently experimented with selecting recruiters based on certain competencies of emotional intelligence. As a result, nearly three times more people were recruited, producing a savings in the cost of recruitment of $3 million annually.

The results were so dramatic that the Secretary of Defense ordered that recruiters in all branches of the service be selected in this way.[4]

A doctoral dissertation on the effectiveness of military teams showed yet another impact of emotional intelligence. Studies of 422 military personnel from 81 teams demonstrated that the emotional intelligence of the team leader was significantly related to the development of emotionally competent group norms, and that these norms resulted in enhanced team performance.[5]

EMOTIONAL INTELLIGENCE AND
HIGH IQ PROFESSIONS

There are many professions that require years of higher education and specialized training for entry into the field. Gaining entrance into educational programs, such as engineering, medical school, or an advanced program in computer sciences, is highly competitive, meaning that only those applicants with the best academic records and performance on standardized entrance exams will make the cut. Getting into intellectually demanding professions suggests that all of those in the field have high IQs or they never would have been admitted into their professional training programs and performed well enough to graduate.

This poses an interesting question. In professions in which everyone has a high IQ and rigorous professional training, what distinguishes those who turn out to be star performers from those who will remain competent but average performers? A fascinating longitudinal study suggests that emotional intelligence makes all the difference. In the 1950s, a group of eighty Ph.D. candidates in scientific fields were chosen for a long-term study at Berkeley. They were given IQ tests, an array of psychological assessments, and intensive interviews.

These scientists were tracked down forty years later when they were all in their 70s. Using a variety of assessment criteria, the researchers rank-ordered the group in terms of their career success and level of prestige in their professional communities. What made the difference? Social and emotional abilities turned out to be four times more important than IQ in determining their overall success.[6]

All these scientists were bright and highly educated people. But IQ and training alone do not a star performer make. Sheer brainpower isn't enough. Those scientists who rose to the top were visionary thinkers who could discipline themselves to focus their energy on what they wanted to accomplish. Their accomplishments also required them to work effectively with other people in securing funding for their projects and building the relationships and teamwork necessary to make the move from vision to producing real results. Social skills play a role in many ways, even in such routine activities as presenting findings at scientific conferences. And while their research studies can stand on their own merits, a social, engaging person is much more likely to build that network of influential relationships that is often necessary to make further progress in their research.

A study at Bell Labs arrived at the same conclusions. The most valued and productive engineers demonstrated greater mastery of emotional intelligence, which turned out to be more important than IQ in determining their overall success. Those who lacked emotional intelligence were found to be critical and condescending, inhibited, and emotionally bland. The most successful engineers were found to be poised and outgoing, sympathetic and caring, and to have rich emotional lives. They were comfortable with themselves and with other people.[7]

EMOTIONAL INTELLIGENCE AND LEADERSHIP

Emotional intelligence plays an essential role in succeeding as a leader. People often get promoted for demonstrating their technical expertise, but it is emotional intelligence that determines how well they will succeed as leaders. Reflecting on your own experience with leaders you've known will tell you this is true. While you must be a master of your professional discipline to succeed in leadership, other personal qualities make the difference in making great leaders.

I've been privileged to work with many great leaders, and the very best of them have common characteristics. They are visionary thinkers who are able to share their vision in a way that inspires others to join them in making it a reality. They are able to build strong teams based on trust and open communications. They set high standards and hold people accountable for meeting up to them. And they have the capacity to convey genuine caring and respect for individuals at all levels of their organizations.

Research confirms the importance of emotional intelligence in leadership. In one study, 300 top-level executives from fifteen global companies were evaluated. Star performers were distinguished by six emotional competencies:

1. Influence
2. Team leadership
3. Organizational awareness
4. Self-confidence
5. Achievement drive
6. Leadership.[8]

A large beverage firm was showing a 50-percent turnover rate of division presidents in their first two years of office, due to poor performance. When the company started hiring on the basis of emotional intelligence, turnover dropped to 6 percent in two years, and 87 percent of the emotionally intelligent division leaders were in the top third of performers as measured by salary bonuses.[9]

When supervisors in a manufacturing plant were trained in emotional competencies—such as empathy and helping employees resolve problems on their own—time lost due to accidents dropped by 50 percent, grievances dropped from 15 to 3 per year, and the plant exceeded its productivity goals by $250,000.[10] Another manufacturing plant provided similar training for supervisors and showed a production increase of 17 percent, with no such increase found in an untrained control group.[11]

The ability to handle stress is another important emotional competency. Store managers in a national retail chain who were best at handling stress outperformed their peers based on net profits, sales per square foot, sales per employee, and per dollar inventory investment.[12]

MATCHING EMOTIONAL INTELLIGENCE TO THE POSITION: THE SIMMONS EQ PROFILE

While the concept of emotional intelligence itself is relatively new, for nearly thirty years Simmons Management Systems has been measuring characteristics that we now put under the heading of emotional intelligence. The Simmons EQ Profile measures thirteen characteristics that provide an unusually accurate insight into how someone can be expected to perform at work:

1. Energy
2. Stress
3. Optimism
4. Self-Esteem
5. Work
6. Detail
7. Change
8. Courage

9. Direction

10. Assertive

11. Tolerance

12. Consideration for Others

13. Sociable

Let us now look at each of these characteristics in greater detail:

1. *Energy.* This is a measure of emotional energy. It is the driver and tells us how much capacity a person has to get things done, withstand stress, and recover from it after a prolonged stress event. This measure tells us whether someone has the emotional drive to succeed in a leadership position or a position demanding a high level of drive to succeed. Unusually low scores on this measure can be an indicator of depression or that the person is experiencing life events, such as a divorce or a serious illness in the family, that are draining their energy and are likely to affect their work performance.

2. *Stress.* This measure is affected by extremely high or low scores on the rest of the Profile. Such extreme scores cause internal stress that affects their ability to perform.

3. *Optimism.* Low scores on optimism predict that someone is gloomy, fault-finding, critical, and blaming of others when things go wrong. A very high score suggests the person is overly trusting and positive, leaving them less likely to identify problems that need to be taken care of.

4. *Self-esteem.* Low self-esteem scores indicate people who have extremely high internal standards and who are likely to be harsh self-critics when they fail to live up to them. High scores indicate a person is putting a good deal of energy into maintaining an outward posture that they feel good about themselves, although inwardly they are more worried than they are willing to reveal. Such people are difficult to coach because they don't want to hear criticism and will

respond defensively and be less willing to acknowledge the need for personal change.

5. *Work.* This is a measure of a person's work ethic and how likely they are to work hard or be less engaged with work.

6. *Detail.* A manager with an overly high detail score is likely to be far too involved in details that are best left to employees to take care of. Extremely low scores on this scale indicate carelessness and inability to attend to detailed work.

7. *Change.* This is a measure of a person's ability to adapt to changing conditions. People with low scores do best with routine and predictable work. A moderately high score indicates that someone works harder when doing work that offers change and variety. Such scores also indicate that the person brings a high degree of creativity in approaching work.

8. *Courage.* This is a measure of orientation to challenge. People in demanding positions need to show moderately high scores on this scale. They do their best when faced with stimulating, challenging work.

9. *Direction.* This assesses a person's ability to size up problems, look at options, and make independent decisions. People with low scores seek out advice and like making decisions as part of a group—not a promising indicator for a leadership role. People with extremely high scores are not only comfortable making decisions, they want to make *all* of them. Leaders with high scores on direction tend to have problems delegating and are often described as "control freaks." This is even more true with people whose detail scores put them into the perfectionist range.

10. *Assertive.* This scale assesses the capacity to make reasonable demands on people, be persuasive, and deal with conflict. Low scores on this scale predict a person will have problems managing people and holding them accountable. Extremely high scores always indicate a harsh, aggressive, and pushy style of communicating that inevitably damages relationships.

11. *Tolerance.* Extremely high scores indicate that people are patient and forgiving to a fault and too slow to react in holding people accountable. Low scores indicate that when something happens that triggers peoples' emotions, they will exaggerate the situation, polarize the positions, and no longer see the situation accurately. A high Assertive score paired with a low Tolerance score indicate a management style that make people very scary bosses.

12. *Consideration for Others.* This score measures empathy and indicates a person's sensitivity to what is going on with other people.

13. *Sociable.* This measure indicates how comfortable people are with others.

While the individual scores in themselves are interesting, in the hands of a trained and experienced interpreter, the overall pattern and interaction of scores result in a very revealing portrait of how a person can be expected to behave in a particular position.

The EQ Profile also offers a variety of norms that assess a person's fit for various levels of management as well as a number of specific types of work such as sales. The company's commitment to continuous research, validation, and the refinement of norms has led to the development of this remarkably accurate assessment device.[13] Users of the instrument give it an accuracy rating of 97 to 100 percent.[14]

The Simmons EQ Profile has been shown to produce tremendous cost savings by assisting companies in matching people to the emotional needs of the job. For example, Methodist Hospitals, in Memphis, Tennessee, had a turnover rate of 65 percent in critical care nurses. Using the EQ Profile as a selection tool, they were able to reduce that turnover rate to 15 percent within 18 months and have kept it at that level for more than 18 years. An in-depth study of the Personal Survey with nurses at that hospital found a correlation of .68 with overall performance.

MAPCO is a large convenience store chain that was struggling with a staggering turnover rate of 171 percent annually. By using the EQ Profile to identify people with the emotional capacities appropriate for that job setting, they were able to reduce turnover to a much more manageable 19 percent, an 89 percent reduction in their annual turnover rate. This produced an annual savings of more than $1,112,000 by reducing the cost of having had to hire and train so many new employees.

Olsten Temporary Services did a study of the correlation of EQ Profile scores with employee rankings in the Olsten's President's Club. The ranking was based on the employees' sales with new and established customers. A multiple regression analysis found a perfect correlation of 1.0. By knowing the person's score on each of the survey's scales they were able to predict the person's job performance at a level of 100 percent.

The Simmons EQ Profile is so sensitive in predicting job performance that it can help companies "clone" employees and leaders. By selecting a group of top performers from a particular position, Simmons can create a customized norm comparison group, enabling companies to hire people with the emotional characteristics known to be critical for success in specific positions.

Nearly 90 percent of NFL draftees take the EQ Profile. Custom norms have been created for various positions because different characteristics are called for in linemen versus quarterbacks, for example. A recent follow-up study with the coaches and advisors of 132 players found that knowing the players' emotional strengths and needs provided them with insights that allowed them to do a better job of tailoring their coaching to match the needs of the individual player.

Not a "One Size Fits All" Assessment

The normative research on the Simmons EQ Profile has demonstrated emotional intelligence is a multidimensional combination of characteristics that must take the demands of the specific job into account to find the right combination of emotional competencies to predict success on the job.

Suppose you want to fill positions that require people to sit at a desk and do highly structured and repetitive work. You want to find people who have moderate energy, a strong work ethic, and high need for detail. You also want these people to like routine work and not have a high need for change and variety. If the work requires few independent decisions, your ideal candidates should not have a high score on direction, indicating that they are comfortable taking directions from others. If these people are required to deal with the public, strong scores on consideration, optimism, and sociability would also be required.

Studies of the various normative groups make clear that different combinations of emotional needs and competencies make people more or less suited to specific jobs. I once had a client looking for someone to lead a highly technical department that was badly out of date in its professional practices and needed to develop a more structured and disciplined approach to its work. The previous leader and his management team took a very lax approach to the management of the division. The organization was succeeding in spite of itself, largely through the efforts of first-line supervisors and some middle managers. Because they were more or less managing themselves, many chose to work on projects that interested them—not necessarily the projects that were essential for the success of the business.

We used the EQ Profile as the key source of information in making the final hiring decision. Interviews identified the top three applicants who were roughly equal in the technical expertise and experience required to reorganize the department and drive the creation of more efficient systems and processes. Given that they were all relatively equal in their qualifications and their ratings in interviews, having an instrument like the EQ Profile turned out to be invaluable in choosing the candidate most likely to succeed in turning the organization around.

Candidate #1 generated a profile suggesting he was a nice guy to a fault. He had moderate energy, work, and detail scores. His Direction scores indicated that he would have problems making independent decisions and that when decisions did get made, they would be made as a group, probably after a good deal of agonizing and wasted time. His Detail score was much too high for a senior executive, suggesting that it would take considerable and time-consuming analysis for him to make a decision. His EQ Profile also revealed extraordinarily high Tolerance, Consideration, and Sociable scores and a very low Assertive score. This man was not strong enough to lead the group through a difficult operational and cultural change. He would have made a nice neighbor but you would never want him to serve as a high-level executive in your organization.

Candidate #2 generated an EQ Profile that was problematic for different reasons. First of all, she had an extremely high emotional Energy score. This was paired with equally high Change and Direction scores. This woman was not just comfortable making decisions, she would probably want to make all of them and get overly involved in micromanaging the organization and not allowing her executives to do their jobs. Moreover, the very high Change score, paired with extremely high Energy, suggested that she would be a moving target. She would want to be in charge but would likely keep changing her mind as to the direction she wanted to go.

The final blow to her candidacy was an extremely high Assertive score paired with very low Tolerance, Consideration, and Sociable scores. This pattern of scores is seen in people whose management style is viewed as harsh and vindictive. When angry, she would tend to exaggerate the problem, polarize positions, and turn issues into black/white, win/lose situations. Her overly high assertiveness and low tolerance would make her a very frightening figure in an organization that needed to be brought together to share a common vision. Finally, her low Sociability score suggested that she would be a very difficult person to warm up to and slow to reveal her values and vision. This company had set as one of its goals to be chosen as one of the best companies in the country to work for. Her EQ Profile scores suggested that she would not help the company make much progress in reaching that goal.

Candidate #3 was much closer to what was required. She had very high Energy and Optimism scores. Those scores, combined with a moderately high Sociability score, suggested she would connect with people easily and bring an upbeat and friendly approach to her leadership that would energize the team she would be leading. Her Work and Detail scores were moderate, as is appropriate for an upper level executive. Her Change score was in the range that suggested that she would be a good change manager and bring a highly creative flair to her thinking. Her Direction score was a little too high but the organization needed someone who would take charge and get the organization moving in the right direction quickly. Once the organization reached a steady operating state, she would have to be coached to delegate and let her direct reports do their jobs. Otherwise, she might have a tendency to be overly involved in decision making.

In the interview, she acknowledged that she was aware of this from her previous position and that it was a trait she was working on moderating. She was appropriately assertive but too low on tolerance, suggesting that she needed to be careful not to exaggerate situations when she was upset or angry. But her Consideration score suggested a healthy degree of empathy, which meant she could be counted on to pick up on it when she was reacting too strongly and putting people off. Of the three top candidates, all of whom were roughly equal in terms of their technical abilities and experience, the EQ Profile identified which candidate had the qualities of emotional intelligence that would predict success.

Candidate #3 has proven to be a good choice. In her first year, she made the changes in the department necessary to make her company more competitive in the marketplace. As predicted, however, she tended to be overly involved in her managers' decisions. They were frustrated by her micromanagement and her tendency to waste time that she should have been investing in the strategic development of her department. She required coaching in delegating enough authority for her executive team to do their jobs.

As these examples make clear, it would be a mistake to think of emotional intelligence as a single factor. There are a number of competencies that fall under the heading of emotional intelligence, and different positions within a company require differing combinations of those competencies to assure success. These competencies are separate dimensions. People can have too little or too much strength on different dimensions, depending on the demands of the job.

Suppose you were coaching someone who is shy and unassertive. His job is to handle customer complaints and resolve any problems appropriately but within guidelines necessary for the financial viability of the product being supported. In coaching him, you would certainly want to work on his empathy skills, making it easier for him to connect with customers and understand their needs. Lacking assertion, this rep would be too likely to replace products with new ones when bringing them in-house via overnight mail would be more economical and still ensure that the customer would have a functioning unit within a short period of time. But in coaching the person to be more assertive and enforce the company's repair policies, the last thing you'd want to do is make him so assertive that he would yell at customers and alienate the customer.

That is the challenge of coaching for emotional intelligence. You are trying to bring certain behaviors or characteristics into a range that is suitable for success on the job. You are dealing with human behavior and sometimes people will overcorrect and go too far in the other direction.

Reflections

1. Technical knowledge and intellectual brilliance are not sufficient to assure success. Have you ever known people who failed

to be anything other than average performers even though their technical abilities and intelligence would seem to predict that these people should be highly successful? What personal competencies—or lack of—seemed to be their saboteurs? Did they lack the ability to translate a great idea into concrete action? Could they remain focused on an idea long enough to do something about it or did they bounce from idea to idea without any organized follow through? Did they lack personal credibility or the interpersonal abilities that would allow them to establish the influence required to build organizational support for their projects?

If you have associates who seem to have sufficient knowledge and intelligence to perform at much higher levels, what are you doing—or failing to do—that contributes to the problem? Up to now, what have you done to make them more successful in their jobs?

2. Think about the people you've worked with over the course of your career. Identify those who were brilliant thinkers and highly knowledgeable in their fields and who were also able to catalyze action in the organization to build support for their ideas.

Make a list of the unique personal and interpersonal qualities that made them so successful in their work. Then evaluate yourself on these same characteristics. Are you meeting the standards set by these outstanding performers or do you need to develop certain qualities of your emotional intelligence to become more effective in your work?

NOTES

1. J. E. Hunter, F. L. Schmidt, and M. K. Judiesch, "Individual Differences in Output Variability as a Function of Job Complexity," *Journal of Applied Psychology* 75 (1990): 28–42.

2. Daniel Goleman, *Working with Emotional Intelligence* (New York: Bantam, 1998).

3. L. M. Spencer Jr. and S. Spencer, *Competence at Work: Models for Superior Performance* (New York: John Wiley and Sons, 1993).

4. General Accounting Office, "Military Recruiting: The Department of Defense Could Improve Its Recruiter Selection and Incentive Systems." Report submitted to Congress in January 1998.

5. Elizabeth Stubbs, *Emotional Intelligence Competencies in the Team and Team Leader: A Multi-Level Examination of the Impact of Emotional Intelligence on Group Performance* (Cleveland: Case Western Reserve University, 2005).

6. G. J. Feist and F. Barron, "Emotional Intelligence and Academic Intelligence in Career and Life Success." Paper presented at the Annual Convention of the American Psychological Society, San Francisco, June 1996.

7. Daniel Goleman, *Utne Magazine,* November/December 1995.

8. L. M. Spencer, Jr., D. C. McClelland, and S. Kelner, *Competency Assessment Methods: History and State of the Art* (Boston: Hay/McBer, 1997).

9. D. C. McClelland, "Identifying Competencies with Behavioral-Event Interviews," *Psychological Science* 9, 5 (1999): 331–339.

10. A. Pesuric and W. Byham, "The New Look in Behavior Modeling," *Training and Development* (July 1996), pp. 25–33.

11. J. I. Porras and B. Anderson, "Improving Managerial Effectiveness Through Modeling-Based Training, *Organizational Dynamics* 9 (1981): 60–77.

12. R. F. Lusch and R. Serpkeuci, "Personal Differences, Job Tension, Job Outcomes, and Store Performance: A Study of Retail Managers, *Journal of Marketing* (1990).

13. Steve Simmons and John C. Simmons, Jr., *Measuring Emotional Intelligence* (Arlington, Tex.: The Summit Publishing Group, 1997).

14. The studies and comments in this section have been provided by the Simmons Management Systems. For more information about the Simmons EQ Profile, contact the author through his website at www.bobwallonline.com.

CHAPTER 3

HOW EMOTIONAL INTELLIGENCE RAISES THE BAR FOR COACHING

WITH THE INCREASING KNOWLEDGE about and emphasis on emotional intelligence, leaders have found that coaching their direct reports has become a great deal more challenging. It used to be enough just to talk about performance standards. Yearly performance measures were established, with an emphasis on nice, clean objectives that were relatively easy to assess and which made it easy to determine whether or not the employee was getting the job done. Any coaching provided throughout the year was based on how well people were making progress in meeting their performance standards.

But with the emergence of emotional intelligence and its impact on success at work, it is no longer enough to talk only about *what* employees are doing. Performance objectives and targets certainly remain important. But leaders must now begin to address the more personal aspects related to *how* people do their work, such as how they get along with their fellow employees. This means talking about behaviors that are linked to character, personality, and how people work with others in doing their jobs.

THE SCARCITY OF COACHING
IN THE WORKPLACE

I used to lead stress management workshops early in my career. At the beginning of every workshop, I'd put people in small groups and ask them this question: "What bugs you about your job?" I'd let them talk for a while. Then we'd make a list of sources of stress on the job.

The bad news for managers? About 90 percent of the items on these lists referred to what the participants' direct managers were doing—or failing to do—that caused needless stress on the job. Certainly, people identified job-related stressors, such as customers who were difficult to please, unpleasant working conditions, or long hours. But most of their complaints focused on their direct managers. And what was the most frequent complaint at the top of the list? "Nobody ever lets me know how I'm doing around here until I screw something up . . . and even then I may not hear about it until my annual evaluation." As one person put it, "Doing a good job around here is like wetting your pants in the dark. It feels warm for a while but no one notices."

Nothing seems to have changed. Over the past twenty years, in project after project, working in all kinds of companies and professions, my private conversations with people reveal that most managers are failing to provide their employees with frequent and effective coaching.

In the absence of hearing from their bosses about the quality of their work, people reach the conclusion that their managers are not paying much attention to what they do and don't care about their performance. In the absence of regular feedback, some people reach wildly inaccurate conclusions about the quality of their work.

Some people assume that they are not doing well. A conversation with a bank vice president revealed she was updating her resume because she felt she was failing to meet her manager's expectations. Why? Because he rarely made any comments about her work and had seemed unusually grumpy around her lately. I suggested she ask him how she was doing before she started looking for other work.

It just so happened that a week or so later that she and her boss were on a business trip to a nearby city. Because she knew the city well, she did the driving. At one point she pulled into a parking lot and said, "I know this city and you don't. If you want to get to our meeting on time, you have to tell me how I am doing at work. You've said so little to me lately that I've begun to wonder if I am in trouble for something you haven't told me about." Her manager began by telling her she was the "consummate professional." He went on to provide examples that made clear he had very high regard for her work. Lately he'd become distracted by issues in his personal and professional life and, as a result, he had been having fewer conversations with her. The combination of inadequate feedback and the increasing sense of disconnectedness from her boss led her to assume that her manager was displeased with her work.

Failure to provide ongoing feedback and coaching can also lead to the exact opposite conclusion, where poor performers may think they are doing just fine. In one project I was told about a manager who had recently gone to his boss to ask for a raise. The conversation ended with the termination of this manager, whose performance had been unacceptable for some time. But in the absence of feedback, he felt that he was doing so well that he deserved a raise!

Assessment interviews in my projects often reveal that someone on a team is not doing a good job and that everyone on the team knows it, but the manager of the team is failing to resolve the problem. In conversations with that person's teammates, they express the opinion that their boss is either oblivious and doesn't notice poor performance or, worse yet, that the boss notices but doesn't care enough to intervene.

The scarcity of praise and inadequate responses to poor performance are difficult to understand. All leaders are accountable for the performance of the teams they lead. This is as true for a first-line supervisor of five people as it is for the president of a company. I've been so puzzled by the low frequency of coaching that I continually ask managers if they feel they are as active as they should be as coaches. Most of the supervisors, managers, and executives I've asked this question admit they could do a better job in this area of their leadership.

They acknowledge that coaching is one of the central responsibilities of their jobs. As well it should be. Whether you are a first-line supervisor or an upper-level executive responsible for a large group of employees, it could be argued that your employees are not doing *their* jobs—they are doing different parts of *your* job for you. As a leader, you are accountable for work done by other people. You are responsible for results that are beyond your capacity to achieve on your own. So you must get your work done by and through other people.

If someone on your team is performing poorly, you have no choice but to intervene and to do so quickly. If you don't, your own manager won't have a problem with that employee—your boss will have a problem with *you*. You are accountable for the performance of each and every person who reports to you. That is what leadership is.

WHY MANAGERS DON'T COACH AS OFTEN AS THEY SHOULD

So why aren't managers responding to performance more often? In exploring why managers don't coach as often as they know they should, I've heard a variety of excuses over the years:

- Many managers are not sure what to say when providing corrective feedback. Their own discomfort with corrective coaching results in uncomfortable conversations, for them and for their employees.

- Others report that some of their employees have reacted emotionally to corrective feedback in the past. As a result, they end up putting off conversations they know they need to have, hoping that the problem will just somehow resolve itself. And, of course, problems left unaddressed only get worse.

- Employees have long wished for more acknowledgments of their efforts. A recent study by the Gallup organization found that two thirds of American workers have not received even a single acknowledgment or thanks from the boss in the past year.[1] The author goes on to reference a study by the U.S. Department of Labor that found the number one reason people leave organizations is that they don't feel appreciated.

- In discussions of praise, some managers say that because their bosses don't praise them, they don't feel the need to praise their own staff.

- Others argue that praise isn't necessary, that people are getting paid for the work they do and that ought to be enough.

- Still others argue that a "No news is good news" approach is sufficient. If employees are not getting yelled at, they should just assume they are doing a good job.

- On some occasions, managers have expressed discomfort with praise, concerned that they might come across as less than genuine and that employees may interpret the praise as manipulative.

- Other managers report that praising someone feels too personal and leaves them feeling uncomfortable. Some even argue that praising people will make them complacent and they'll stop working so hard.

- Some managers are afraid that if they praise people they will ask for a raise. So they withhold praise to avoid that conversation.

- Lack of time is clearly an issue that gets in the way of coaching. Managers are busy people. They might go to work in the morning determined to speak with someone about their performance, but in the rush to get everything else done, they don't find the time to for those kinds of conversations.

THE IMPACT OF EMOTIONAL INTELLIGENCE AND COACHING PROVIDED BY MANAGERS

As we begin our exploration of how emotional intelligence has made coaching all the more challenging, let's refine our definition of coaching:

Coaching is a structured conversation designed to enhance, maintain, improve, or correct performance.

That is all coaching is—a conversation about performance. When I talk with managers about coaching, the topic generates an emotional response suggesting that they have overcomplicated the topic. It conjures up memories of awkward moments when they didn't know what to say, or times when the employees disagreed with their coaching and conversations spiraled out of control. Most managers agree that they should do much more coaching but because they lack a simple model for coaching effectively and comfortably, they put it off and even withhold it until the annual performance appraisal. You can only imagine how much both managers and employees look forward to annual conversations that happen only because company policies require it.

PERFORMANCE MANAGEMENT VS. COACHING FOR EMOTIONAL INTELLIGENCE

As noted in the beginning of this chapter, the topic of emotional intelligence has made management coaching far more challenging than simply addressing performance objectives. Emotional intelligence refers to a variety of personal and interpersonal competencies that have a huge impact on a person's success at work. Coaching must now include personal qualities and interpersonal effectiveness that address *how* people go about doing *what* they are expected to do. It must now address issues such as a person's inability to get organized and get things done, shyness and reluctance to speak up in meetings, problems with anger that lead to damaged relationships with coworkers or customers, personal habits or interpersonal quirks that put people off, and other issues that may be damaging someone's interpersonal effectiveness on the job.

In sum, coaching must now include aspects of an employee's performance that may be deeply personal, as well as challenging to describe clearly. Coaching for emotional intelligence requires leaders to develop a much more intimate approach to their coaching, addressing behaviors that limit the employee's ability to build relationships and establish influence. The prospect of doing this kind of coaching makes many managers feel inadequate and uncomfortable.

As the research on emotional intelligence and success at work so clearly demonstrates, helping employees develop certain personal and interpersonal competencies can produce a dramatic improvement in *what* people accomplish as they become more effective in *how* they go about getting it done.

I've had so many conversations about coaching in my career that I can say this with dead certainty: People want their leaders to notice what they do, to offer appreciation for work well done, and to provide timely and appropriately phrased corrective coaching when improvement in performance is needed. If you do the exercises and master the coaching strategies and skills presented in this book, you will produce a dramatic increase in your comfort and effectiveness as a coach. You will also discover that coaching for emotional intelligence can result in personal growth that changes the lives of your employees as well as enhances their performance.

Reflections

1. On a scale of 1 to 10, how would you rate the frequency and effectiveness of your corrective coaching?

2. On a scale of 1 to 10, how would you rate the frequency and effectiveness of the praise, acknowledgment, and gratitude you express to people on your team for work well done?

3. If you rated yourself any lower than 10 on either question, what changes do you need to make to become the coach you know you want to be?

4. How do you feel about praise? Do you have any beliefs or assumptions about praise that keep you from praising or expressing thanks to each member of your team at least once a week?

5. If you could learn a method of offering acknowledgment that takes only 15 seconds, would you do so more often? If so, how do you think this would affect your team's morale and productivity?

6. If you avoid or delay corrective coaching, what message are you sending to the members of your team?

7. If you allow someone to persist in performing at an unacceptable level, how does this affect the rest of the team?

8. Corrective feedback can be delivered in about 45 seconds. This method can be used to nip problems in the bud as well as respond to performance or behavior that is clearly unacceptable. You can also use this approach to help people grow and develop. They may already be performing at an acceptable level but you can help them improve their skills and become even better at what they do.

9. Reflect for a moment about each member of your team. In what ways would more active coaching raise the morale and overall performance effectiveness of your team?

10. Are you willing to invest a little time and effort to have that level of impact on your team?

NOTE

1. Tom Rath, "The Best Ways to Recognize Employees," *Gallup Management Journal,* December 9, 2004.

CHAPTER 4

COACHING AND THE DIVERSITY
OF THE HUMAN EXPERIENCE

THERE IS A GREAT DEAL OF WORK being done on the impact of diversity in the workplace. For good reason. Factors such as race, ethnicity, country of origin, age, and gender can lead to differences in our life experiences that influence our development. Understanding these differences helps us understand each other and learn how to work better together.

Even so, I believe we are far more diverse than can be accounted for by the more obvious differences among us. Each of us has our own unique story—a series of life events that shaped our perceptions of ourselves and what we think is possible for us in life. Every person you will ever work with brings to the workplace a unique personal history of events that has shaped her as a human being. Each person's history has had a dramatic impact on the unfolding and development of his emotional intelligence. If you are going to coach people to develop their emotional intelligence, you have to remember we human beings have so much in common yet we are so different.

Lynn's model of emotional intelligence, as outlined in Chapter

1, has five broad components: mastery of purpose and vision; self-awareness and self-control; empathy; social expertness; and personal influence. Each of these capacities begins to take form from the early days of our lives and continues to develop throughout the rest of our lives.

THE INFLUENCE OF GENETICS

Even before we are born, we are different from our peers. Genetics plays a huge role in creating diversity among human beings. It determines native IQ. You are born with a certain IQ, whether 90 or 145, and that's the way it is. There isn't much you can do to make a genius out of someone who was born with an IQ of 95. IQ plays an important role in how well we do in school. How well we do in school has a great deal to do with how we feel about ourselves and what we begin to define as possible for us in life.

Genetics also plays a role in shaping our personality. Heredity has been shown to have an influence on our degree of introversion/extraversion, agreeableness/aggression, conscientiousness, and optimism/pessimism.[1] Being born predisposed to certain traits does not necessarily mean people are fated to live with those traits the rest of their lives. Circumstances, events, and important people in our lives will play a role in shaping how fully we express or overcome these inborn traits. Other interests and talents may also be influenced by genetics. For example, some people seem to be born with the capacity to develop certain abilities at a rate that far exceeds that of the general population. Some people seem to have been born to be artists or musicians. Even physical attractiveness and height is being shown to have an impact on how we are perceived and how successful we become. The point is that the topic of diversity is a lot more complicated than race or ethnicity. We come out of the womb with a unique combination of genes that will have a great deal to do with how we turn out as adults.

GROWING UP IN A SMALL TOWN

I am going to share some of the early events and circumstances that played a role in making me the person I am today. As you read my story, think about your own. What influences made you the person you are today? What people played a positive or negative role in shaping your sense of yourself and limited or expanded what you thought was possible for you in life? Think about the people who report to you. What life circumstances and events might have played a role in developing the people who report to you today? Would understanding these circumstances make it easier for you to be compassionate and supportive in coaching them?

I was born and grew up in a very small Midwestern town. From the vantage point of someone who might do diversity training, my hometown was as about as bland and homogeneous as you can imagine. Everyone in town was white and either Protestant or Catholic. Almost everyone could be considered middle class. Fathers worked. Most mothers stayed home and took care of the family. We had one movie theater in town. There was Little League, swimming, and detasseling corn in the summer, and basketball, sledding, and skating on the lake in the winters.

You would think that people growing up in a town like this would be as alike as cookies coming off the assembly line. Yet even in that tiny little town, my peers and I grew up learning very different lessons about ourselves, lessons that were to reverberate throughout the rest of our lives.

The Influence of Family of Origin

In spite of all the outward similarities of the people in my hometown, children were born into very different families. The qualities found in these families played a huge role in our early formative experiences. Some parents were loving and nurturing. Others were harsh and punitive. Still others had cold and distant relationships with each other and their children. Some families encouraged self-discovery and self-expression. Others responded harshly to anything that hinted of disagreement with parental dictates and values.

Even before going to school, the quality of our family lives played a huge role in shaping our views of who we were and what was possible for us in life. We began to develop very different styles of communication and coping strategies for getting along and getting our needs met. Some of us learned to be direct and straightforward. Others learned to lie and manipulate. Some found that withdrawal, pouting, and looking unhappy eventually got them what they wanted. Still others learned that it was dangerous to disagree with authority figures. By the time children reached school age, their self-concepts were already well on the way to being formed. Some felt the world was a safe and friendly place. Others learned that life was filled with danger and potential punishment.

The Power of Peer Groups and Authority Figures

Then we were exposed to other adults—in school, religious organizations, and in activities for children run by adults. Adults who played significant roles in our lives added yet more lessons about ourselves, which we internalized. Even in that small Midwestern town, my peers and I were each exposed to an infinite variety of experiences that were uniquely our own, and which played a huge role in developing the adults we would one day become. We developed our own views of the world and what we thought we could accomplish in it. We learned different methods of coping with feelings and ways of expressing our needs. And we developed our own unique sense of self.

Every person you ever work with or manage brings with him his own history that has shaped the adult you see in front of you. When I think of how incredibly diverse we are as individuals, I am sometimes amazed that organizations work as well as they do. Teams are made up of individuals, each of whom is a product of her own unique blend of experiences that have shaped her attitudes, opinions, beliefs, and communication strategies and skills. Yet in spite of our diversity, we manage to work well together most of the time.

FORMATIVE CIRCUMSTANCES
AND EXPERIENCES

Some of the early events and circumstances that shaped the person we were to become were so powerful that we may not even recognize their impact until years later in our adulthood. I want to share two of the defining experiences that were central in my forming of the self I carried into adulthood. Again, as you read my story, be thinking about those defining circumstances that affected your development and may yet still play a role in how you are as an adult to this very day.

Learning to Avoid Conflict

Among the host of variables affected by genetics are two that are very important in the shaping of personalities: introversion/extroversion and optimism/pessimism. I was born an introverted pessimist. I probably came out of the womb worried that the nurse wouldn't know how to cut the cord properly but of course I couldn't find the courage to say anything about it. From a very early age, I took life very, very seriously. Had I gone to the public school in town, this combination of characteristics might not have been such a problem. In a larger school, I would have found other kids like myself to hang out with.

But I went to a very small Catholic school and there were between twenty-five and thirty students in my classes as I grew up. Only six of us were boys. Five of them were normal, athletic, rough and tumble boys. Then there was me. I was shy, introverted, studious, and I took life so very seriously. I wore glasses and braces. I was overly sensitive and cried easily. Feeling alienated from my peers, I tried very hard to please adults. Every class has the kid whom everyone picks on and makes fun of, and I was the one. From my late grade school years through high school, I was the butt of jokes. Children and teenagers can be amazingly cruel.

I learned to cope with the teasing and harassment by not responding. Getting upset only brought me more unwanted attention so I did my best to show no outward reaction. To pull this off, I'd say things to myself like, "It doesn't mean anything. Don't make a big deal out of it." I became very adept at denial and not giving my tormentors the satisfaction of a visible response. I knew that to do so would only result in more teasing.

Years later, in my late 40s, I took the Simmons EQ Profile for the first time. A friend and colleague of mine, Wes Crane, had already been using it in his consulting for years. My life at the time was in crisis, both personally and professionally. Although I am a psychologist by training, I was taught to approach all assessment devices with deep skepticism. I learned how difficult it is to design an assessment instrument that actually does what it claims to do. At Wes's urging, I took the Profile, but with little expectation it would produce much of any interest.

I'll never forget Wes's interpretation of my Profile. Wes described someone I'd fire if he worked for me and one whom I would certainly never hire. My first reaction was to reject the results, but after cooling down, I realized that all I had to do was look at my business results: It was all there on the Profile report.

But there was a pattern of results I argued strongly could not be true of me. My Profile indicated that I put so much emphasis on smooth, conflict-free relationships that there would be times I would sell out on my own values and standards. I considered myself an expert in conflict management. I had created strategies and communications skills to deal with conflict. I had trained hundreds of people in those skills. I had written about them. To be told I was unassertive when the chips were down was a complete violation of my self-concept.

Rather than argue with me, Wes was wise enough to encourage me to suspend judgment and observe myself for a while before discounting the scores. About a month later, I had an appointment with a client who did not show up. It was a busy traffic day in Seattle. I drove for an hour to get to his office and waited for 45 minutes. It was now rush hour and the drive home took well over 90 minutes. I had wasted a whole afternoon. I was more than a little irritated that my client hadn't shown up.

When I saw my client a week later, he did what you'd expect him to do. He started to describe the chain of events that led to his missing the meeting and forgetting to call me about his change of schedule. I'll never forget that moment. I had something akin to an "out of body" experience. I observed myself sitting there thinking, "Oh, its no big deal. These things happen. People sometimes mix up their calendars. Don't make a big thing out of it. It's okay."

I caught myself in mid-thought and realized that I was doing exactly what the EQ Profile said I would do. It was not okay with me that he missed the meeting. I had wasted a Friday afternoon. Work that was due by Monday I had ended up doing on Saturday, which meant it cost me part of my weekend. I was really quite irritated and inconvenienced by the missed appointment. Yet there I sat, minimizing the issue and waltzing around how I really felt about the wasted time. So I took a deep breath and said, "We were scheduled to meet. I was here and you weren't. I am going to bill you for my time." My client understood and we moved on.

Then I began to observe myself very closely. At times I was assertive. But on other occasions I would react to something in the situation and back away from expressing myself fully. I might have been responding to the prestige of the other person. Or the conversation had an emotional charge that I wanted to avoid.

I started to be alert for any form of the thought, "Don't make a big deal out of this. It is okay. Don't make a fuss about this." Such thoughts became a red flag, alerting me to do a "gut check." In the heat of the moment, I would ask myself if this was really okay with me or was I about to wimp out again?

As I became more self-aware of my tendency to avoid certain conflicts, I started catching myself in the act of avoiding conflict in the heat of the moment before it was too late. I worked on saying what was really on my mind. Within a year, my business doubled. My marketing became more effective. My consulting certainly improved as I started living up to my value that I would tell the truth, even if I ran the risk of losing the job.

In my childhood, I had learned to deal with teasing by using the response of not responding. I'd learned that skill so well that I was still doing it in my 40s. It was costing me clients and damaging my business. I also looked back on a series of events in my personal life in which I felt taken advantage of or victimized. I could now see that I had allowed those events to happen by not standing up for myself.

This single new awareness of myself created a turning point in my life. I had acquired a habitual avoidance of conflict in my youth and it had become invisible to me, like software running in the background. By avoiding "danger," I was limiting my own success in life and I was oblivious to the pattern of thought that was so self-defeating. Unless we are self-aware, we cannot see what patterns of behaviors need correction.

One of your major goals in coaching for emotional intelligence is to raise people's self-awareness of patterns of behavior that damage their effectiveness at work. I have often found in executive coaching that creating self-awareness of a limiting pattern of thinking or behavior is about 85 percent of the work in helping someone make a significant change. Once clients see themselves clearly, they may need to do little more than to identify the chain of thoughts and feelings that precedes the behavior. As they start catching themselves in the act of doing "it" again, they can make a conscious choice to behave more appropriately.

Feeling Like I Just Didn't Fit In

Most of my childhood I just felt like I didn't fit in. In fact, I didn't. I was overly serious and introspective. I was shy, self-conscious, and at a complete loss for how to start a conversation. In general, I got along better with adults than kids my own age. I also related to girls as friends much better than with the boys in my class. Girls had actual conversations that interested me. But guy talk was something I never did learn to do very well.

My first Communion, a very big event in the life of a Catholic child, took place in second grade. I was deeply moved by the experience. I was dumb enough to ask the other guys if they felt tearful as we were going into the church that Sunday morning. Bad move. I took teasing about that one for weeks to come. More and more, I was learning to shut down and not talk about internal thoughts and feelings that were important to me.

The feeling of not fitting in, particularly with men, followed me into my adulthood. All the years of being teased and made to feel like an outcast had done lasting damage to my confidence and ease around people. But I always spoke well in front of groups and would at times find myself asked to take on a leadership role in activities I was engaged in. I twice served as the president of the Seattle Choral Company. At the break during rehearsal, I would get up in front of the group and make announcements and handle other topics needed for the chorus to function. But during the break, I would walk purposefully in and out of the room, looking like I had things to do. But the truth is painful to admit. I was too shy and uncomfortable with people to be able to approach them and start a conversation.

The feeling of not fitting in was not a major problem for my career. The consulting relationship has a structure and defined roles that made it easy for me to work with people. I knew how to do my job and do it well. But I had trouble making small talk during breaks. In meeting prospective clients for the first time, I am sure that I gave people a first impression that belied the years of experience I bring to my consulting. I knew this was something I had to work on.

I went to workshops of various kinds and read a number of books on how to socialize and to make conversation. I will probably never be as good at it as many people are, but I've made huge progress in this area. One thing I discovered was that I had to pay less attention to my internal monologue and show more interest in other people. Smile, introduce myself, ask how people are doing, and then *listen and respond* to what they have to say. I am still working on connecting with people. Some habits formed early in life take a lifetime of conscious work to overcome. But it can be done. I've made a great deal of progress and I keep working on it to this day.

EVERYONE HAS A STORY

When you lead people, you must remember the importance of an individual's life experiences. Some people were blessed with great parents. Others had parents who inflicted great damage—emotional, if not physical. They may have taught them inappropriate methods of communicating. Or they may have treated them in ways that had a devastating impact on their self-esteem and what they thought was possible for them in their lives. Their early experiences with peer groups affected them positively or negatively. Significant adults in their lives may have empowered them or undermined their confidence and created a fear of anyone in authority. They may have faced serious illness, the loss of a loved one, or other trauma.

When you start coaching for emotional intelligence, never forget such factors. Until you understand the person, it will be difficult for you to coach someone to develop emotional intelligence.

Reflections

1. List the two most important events or circumstances in your life that had a negative impact on your performance as an adult. It may be something you are struggling with to this day.

- Describe the events or circumstances and how these shaped the adult you are today.
- List the ways these aspects of your history are affecting your performance in a negative way.
- Identify "red flags" that will help you become more self-aware of assumptions, beliefs, emotions, or behaviors that limit your effectiveness. Which "red flags" are clues that you are about to "do it" again (whatever your "it" happens to be)?
- Create an action plan. When you start catching yourself in the act of an old, unwanted behavior or reaction, what can you say to yourself to redirect your thinking and behave more effectively before it is too late?
- Don't be discouraged if you backslide. You may be changing a behavior that has formed over a lifetime of experiences. Just keep catching yourself in the act and trying out new behaviors. You do have a choice. You can make significant changes. All it takes is practice. In time, the new behavior will become strong enough to replace the old.

2. List three ways in which you were blessed by circumstances or events as you were growing up. In what ways have they made you a better person today?

3. Make a list of those who report to you. In evaluating their emotional intelligence, what life circumstances can you imagine that might have affected them in a positive or negative way? Do you have the quality of relationship with them that they would feel comfortable talking about significant life events that were instrumental in shaping the people they are today?

4. Review the Reflections exercises in Chapter 1. You may also find it useful to discuss many of these exercises and questions with your employees, as you get to know them better. You might be surprised by what you will learn about people in conversations about their vision, values, life aspirations, and the critical formative experiences in their lives. These conversations will also pro-

vide you with clues in discovering the best approach for coaching each of the unique human beings who reports to you.

NOTE

1. Thomas J. Bouchard, Jr., "Genetic Influence on Human Psychological Traits," *Current Directions in Psychological Science* 13, 4 (2004): 148–151.

PART II

COACHING FUNDAMENTALS

CHAPTER 5

PERSONAL CONNECTIONS: LAYING THE FOUNDATION FOR COACHING

THE RESPONSIBILITY AND AUTHORITY to coach comes with your position as the leader of a team. You tell people what to do. If they don't do it, the organization will allow you to apply negative consequences, such as a letter of reprimand. In addition, as the team leader, there are other, more informal actions you can take to let people know that you are not pleased with them. You can exclude them from plum assignments, cut them out of meetings, or give them the tasks no one else wants to do. You can treat people in such a way as to make clear that you do not like them and would just as soon they go work somewhere else.

In years long past, this kind of leadership may have been acceptable. For an entire generation of people who grew up during the Depression, having a job was reward enough in its own right. It didn't matter if they liked the job or how they were treated. As long as they were able to bring in a reliable wage to support the family, that was good enough. As a young boy in the 1950s, I can remember my father telling me, "You will earn your bread by the sweat of your brow." His attitude toward work was that work was exactly that: Work was work and you didn't have to like it. You just had to do it. That's what a "real man" does.[1]

Years ago, the *Phil Donahue Show* did a program about work. One of the guests, a street musician, described a policeman approaching him one day and asking him why he didn't go get a job. The musician replied that every day, rain or shine, he stood on a specific corner, put out his guitar case, and proceeded to play and sing all day long. As people passed by, they would listen for a time and leave a dollar or two in his guitar case. He told the policeman that this was his job; that this was how he supported himself. The policeman looked at him and said, "This isn't work. You *like* it."

WORK AND LEADERSHIP IN THE INDUSTRIAL AGE

That story captures a dramatic shift that has taken place in the American workplace over the last few generations. America's economy used to be based on industrial production. Thousands of people worked long hours in factories, standing on assembly lines and doing the same thing over and over and over again. The company determined how things were done and defined each worker's role in the process. As long as each person did exactly what he was told to do at the proper pace, raw materials and parts came in at one end of the factory and completed products came out at the other.

For a long time, this worked and made America the world's leading industrial power. Looking back, it is easy to focus on the abuses of the sweatshops, union busting, and child labor. But the industrial age made the dreams of thousands of immigrants come true. America was seen as the land of opportunity, and European economic conditions offered little hope for those wanting to support their families. So immigrants swarmed to America in search of work. The melting pot of American culture also meant that we were a country of many languages.

Looking back on it from our perspective today, life at work in that era looks brutish, even cruel. But think about it from the perspective of people of those times. The American factory, with management making all the decisions and people just doing what they were told to do, was indeed for many people the realization of the American dream. With massive production processes broken down into simple repetitive elements, and with each worker doing their assigned tasks all day long, the job got done. As long as each person did their part, it wasn't even necessary for this multilingual workforce to even talk to each other. As hard as those times might have been, the industrial age in America did provide immigrants with the dignity of a job and the ability to support families in ways that were unimaginable "back in the old country."

What was the "leadership principle" of that age? Either come to work on time and do what you are told or we'll find someone who will. Supervisors, or whatever they were called back then, rode herd over the process. Middle managers, lacking today's information technology, tracked all the numbers and laboriously produced the information that allowed upper management and owners to run their organizations.

SWEEPING CHANGE: LEADERSHIP IN THE INFORMATION AGE

The last sixty years have produced a sea change in the world's workplace. In the age of technology, we now hire people for their knowledge, skills, and brainpower rather than for their muscles and sweat.

This has produced a revolution in what is expected of leaders at all levels of the organization. Shortly after World War II, you probably would have had to look long and hard to find more than a few books on management and leadership. Now the library shelves are filled with hundreds of books about organizational and leadership theories that were the rage for a short time, only to be replaced by new models and paradigms about how organizations should be structured and function, and about what would be required to lead people successfully in those environments.

While organizational theory continues to evolve and change at an ever increasing rate, there is one sure and certain conclusion to be reached about how the technological and information age has affected leaders at all levels of today's organizations:

> It is no longer enough for leaders to give people resources and tell them what to do. Today's leader must be adept at creating a culture of relationships that encourages thinking, creativity, and participation in making companies successful. To accomplish this, leaders must *earn* the ability to influence what people think about, what they value, and how they express those values in the decisions they make from day to day.

In today's workplace, position and authority are not enough in themselves to endow leaders with real influence over the workforce. Certainly, leaders still have clout. Even to this day, some rely on their authority to use punishment as a method of motivating people to produce results. Managing people through fear and intimidation does not work with people who were hired for their knowledge and creativity. With the information age, the culture of work has changed in several significant ways:

• Workers are no longer cogs in the machinery. In modern companies, people aren't given a simple assembly-line-like role whereby they perform tasks over and over again. Today's workforce operates with a better understanding of the company's overall vision and strategic goals and is expected to bring their brainpower to bear on achieving those goals. Leaders at each level of the organization must understand the company's broad purpose, vision, values, and goals and be able to communicate them so that every person in the organization knows how the work they are doing contributes to the overall success of the company.

• People are hired for their training, experience, and brainpower and they are expected to think and to bring their ideas for improvement, innovation, and increased efficiencies to the table for discussion. Collaborative teamwork marked by a free and open expression of ideas is the norm in today's business environment.

• Collaborative teamwork is a product of leadership. Team members will not share ideas or disagree with or question decisions that don't make sense to them, unless the leader of the team has the emotional intelligence required to build an atmosphere of trust and openness that encourages the expression of every person's point.

• Collaborative teamwork requires that each member of the team be an expert in his or her field of technical expertise. But technical expertise alone is not enough. Today's workers must also exhibit the degree of emotional intelligence required to work collaboratively with their coworkers.

• If leaders see people behaving in ways that suppress collaboration, that alienate people in the organization, or that makes them less effective than they need to be, they have no choice but to provide coaching that will help people make the necessary improvements. As we have seen, this is difficult. It is one thing to provide feedback on a missed deadline or quality of work that is unacceptable. It is quite another to provide coaching on issues that are related to a person's character, self-discipline, and interpersonal effectiveness.

CAN COACHING HAVE AN IMPACT ON EMOTIONAL INTELLIGENCE?

This is a question worth asking. It could be argued that certain behaviors and traits are inborn and formed over a lifetime of experience. Is it realistic for a leader to expect to provide coaching that will make subtle or even dramatic changes in what might be thought of as personality traits? Obviously, my answer is "Yes," or I would not have written this book. However, the coaching will be only as effective as the person providing the coaching.

Some may question whether dysfunctional behaviors related to emotional intelligence might best be left to therapists. If the behaviors addressed in coaching can be linked to a person's success on the job, almost anything is open for discussion. Your job as a coach is to help people perform on the job. You may have people on your team whose lack of self-confidence makes them reluctant to speak up in meetings, especially when senior managers are present. Or you may be coaching people who disrupt team meetings with inappropriate displays of anger.

Certainly these are traits that would affect their personal lives as well. But for our purposes, you will learn how to focus on the impact of these patterns of communication only as it applies to their professional effectiveness. Coaching for emotional intelligence is not therapy. You will learn how to keep the focus of these conversations where they belong: on the person's performance at work and the limiting impact certain behaviors may have on his ability to get work done with and through other people.

This is not personal. It is professional, and you have a responsibility to help your direct reports be everything they can be. But a surprising—and deeply gratifying—thing will happen as you improve your skills in coaching for emotional intelligence. You'll find that the coaching you provide at work will produce a ripple effect that can have a profound impact on peoples' lives outside of work. People don't behave one way at work and turn into different people when they go home. So while your intention is to help employees interact more effectively at work with their coworkers, don't be surprised if some come back and thank you for helping them work on shortcomings that have made them better spouses or parents. I know. I've heard this time and again from my clients.

FIVE REQUIREMENTS FOR EFFECTIVE COACHING

To be effective in coaching for emotional intelligence requires that you exhibit and master the following behaviors:

1. Continuous improvement of your own emotional intelligence
2. Personal mastery of vision and values
3. Strong personal relationships with your direct reports
4. Frequent spontaneous coaching
5. Structured conversations when spontaneous coaching doesn't get the job done

Continuous Improvement of Your Own Emotional Intelligence

To provide coaching for emotional intelligence, you must become a student of the topic and start developing those aspects of your own emotional competencies that need improvement. You will hardly be a credible coach if you don't model the very behaviors you are asking people to develop.

This is not as easy as it may seem. Most of us have blind spots, that is, flaws in our own characters that probably developed early in life and are so much a part of us that we don't even see them in ourselves. But when I interview workplace team members, it is very clear that these character flaws are painfully obvious to everyone else on the team.

I've learned that most people have good intentions most of the time. Can you imagine people waking up in the morning and asking themselves, "What can I do to undermine the morale and productivity of my team today? I know what to do. I'll be irritable and yell at someone in the staff meeting. Then I'll look angry and unapproachable the rest of the day. That ought to do it."

Many leaders go to work and undermine morale and productivity, but rarely because of a conscious decision to do so. They are doing what they know how to do. It seems to work for them, and no one tells them to behave differently. So they continue to do it. But when provided with direct feedback on their behavior and how it is affecting others, many are surprised to hear how others see them and actually are embarrassed by how their behavior has been affecting others.

As you learn more about providing better coaching for your direct reports, you will start to catch yourself in the act of behaving in ways that indicate a need for improvement in your own emotional competencies. In time you'll discover that you are making personal changes because you have been paying more attention to displays of emotional intelligence among your staff.

Being more open to learning about yourself as you study emotional intelligence is very important. A recent study reported findings that upper level executives have inflated views of themselves when it comes to emotional intelligence. Comparing self-ratings with ratings provided by people who work with and for them, executives rated themselves as much more competent in emotional intelligence than did people who worked with them frequently and knew them quite well.[2] For years, I have been gathering information about managers and executives in private interviews. Upper level leaders are often dismayed by the marked discrepancies between their perceptions of themselves versus how they are perceived by the rest of the organization. As painful as it is for them to get this kind of feedback, their increasing self-awareness opens the door to personal change.

Personal Mastery of Vision and Values

Mastery of vision and values begins with declaring your vision and values. There are two levels to take into consideration. First, your company probably has a mission statement and a statement of core values. Every leader in the organization must consider how well they are personally living up to both. Does the organization's statement have meaning? Is it translated into action every day? Are decisions made that are congruent with the organization's stated purpose and values? And, especially important, to the extent that the values address how people inside the organization are to be treated, is the leadership team delivering on their promises? Even one visible leader being allowed to remain in the organization in spite of treating people in ways that are a gross violation of the company's stated values creates cynicism within the organization.

A few years ago, I was doing an organizational development project for a Fortune 500 company. During a break between assessment interviews, I went to the coffee room. There on the wall was a nicely produced bronze plaque with a statement of the company's cultural values. When I noticed a couple of employees standing near the coffee pot, I pointed to the plaque and asked them what they thought of it. Both of them laughed, but it was laughter with an edge of bitterness. One of them said, "Management went off on retreat and produced that. But it doesn't mean anything. Nobody lives up to it."

When I work with executive teams on mission and corporate values, I caution them that this kind of work is never neutral. Stated values represent promises being made to the organization. Most organizations have values proclaiming that their associates are their greatest assets. Their values may go on to describe how these associates will be treated. Typically, that they will be treated with respect and that management listens to the people who do the job. Some values proclaim that the culture of the organization will provide a nurturing and supportive environment in which all employees are encouraged to develop to their fullest potential.

When these organizations have leaders whose behavior is clearly out of sync with the company's stated values and nothing is done about it, all it does is create greater cynicism and even despair in the rest of the organization. Executive teams shouldn't even consider doing this kind of vision-and-values work unless they are willing to take an honest look at their culture and assess every member of the leadership team. Such values should never be shared with associates until every manager is either walking the talk or has been replaced by someone who does.

In addition to the corporate mission and values, every leader should have a personal vision statement and a list of core values. I urge you to do and commit to writing the Reflections exercises at the end of this chapter. Then, as you'll see, these values can be shared with your direct reports, putting you on the hook for following through and living up to your words.

Strong Personal Relationships with Your Direct Reports

You cannot hold yourself at a personal distance and still build the personal influence that will allow you to be an effective coach of emotional intelligence. Note the use of the words "personal relationship." That does not mean that you have the same kind of relationship you might have with a close friend outside of work.

There are different levels of intimacy, and you want your relationship with your direct reports to be appropriate to the workplace. That does not mean that you share every intimate detail of your life with them. But it does mean reaching out and establishing contact with people at a personal level. It means getting to know people and what is important to them. You learn about their aspirations, their dreams, and their families.

This is a two-way street. You must let people get to know you as well. You can talk about your vision and values. You can share something you've read that inspired you recently. You let people know about your professional history and important events that shaped the progress of your career. You may talk about leaders who have been influential in your development and what qualities these people had that touched you. And you share enough details about your personal life so that people can feel a sense of connection with the person behind the role you play in their lives.

I have been dismayed at how often I've heard people in leadership positions assert that you have to hold yourself at a distance to manage people well. Some go so far as to say, "I don't have to be liked. I just want to be respected." These managers often treat people in ways that they end up being neither liked nor respected.

I've come to believe that managers who hold themselves at a distance are taking the easy way out. They don't have to invest time or emotion in developing relationships. They don't "waste" time in coaching and development. If they have to fire people or lay people off, they don't have the emotional connections that can make these actions so personally difficult.

A personal connection with your associates is essential in earning the personal influence required to coach for emotional intelligence. Remember, people need to know that you genuinely care about them and that you have their best interests at heart. They want to know that you pay attention to what they do and that you appreciate the effort they make to make you and your team look good. They also want to know that you support them attaining their personal and professional goals. This means providing them with feedback on their performance on a regular basis.

Let me remind you why developing relationships with your direct reports is so important. When you coach for emotional intelligence, you will be touching on issues that are deeply personal but nonetheless have an important impact on a person's success at work. You have to build a bond of trust, caring, and personal connectedness with people to succeed in providing coaching on some of the topics we'll be discussing later on in this book.

Frequent Spontaneous Coaching

People need to know that you are paying attention to what they do and that they can count on frequently hearing from you regarding what you appreciate about their performance as well as how they can improve. Coaching needs to be something that becomes a routine part of your relationships with people, rather than an occasional conversation when someone makes a glaring error or makes an outstanding contribution that demands recognition.

You will learn how to praise someone effectively in about 15 to 20 seconds. Corrective feedback takes a little longer and may sometimes even lead to a short conversation. You will need to include a great deal more praise than given by most managers I've seen in my career. You should praise or say thanks to each of your direct reports at least once a week. Acknowledgment lets people know that you are paying attention to their performance and that you appreciate their efforts. It also accomplishes something else. If people are used to getting positive feedback from you on a regular basis, it makes them more open and receptive to your corrective coaching.

Structured Conversations When Spontaneous Coaching Doesn't Get the Job Done

Because most people want to do a good job, frequent praise and corrective feedback is all it takes to help people keep growing and get better at what they do. On occasion, you may run into employees who do not respond to your coaching. If their performance or interpersonal relationships are proving to be a serious detriment to the work that needs to get done, you will have to bring a more rigorous and disciplined approach to your coaching.

This book includes worksheets for gathering observations and organizing them for serious conversation intended to turn the employee around. You will also find a method for structuring the conversation to make sure you maintain control over the conversation and have the greatest chance of producing your desired outcome.

Reflections

1. Have you or your company ever fired someone due to behavior that was clearly inconsistent with the company's stated values? Has this ever happened? Does it need to happen now?

2. If you are an executive, do you have managers who need coaching to bring them in line with the company's values? Have you provided this coaching? If not, what message are you sending the rest of the organization about the importance of these values?

3. Do you have metrics that allow you to track the quality of culture in each of the teams in your organization? If not, get your associates involved in establishing simple measures to track quarterly. Pose this question: If we were to work together to create the ideal work environment that would allow you to work at your best while finding satisfaction in your work, what measures would we need to track regularly to move in the direction of creating that culture?

4. Does your upper management team have a structured format for its meetings that includes the identification of "talking points" that must be shared with all associates after every meeting?

5. Does your company have a mission statement and stated corporate values? How often do you refer to your company's mission

or values statements in making decisions and sharing those decisions with your team?

6. What are your beliefs, attitudes, and assumptions regarding establishing personal relationships with people on your team? Do your relationships with your associates let them know that you are interested in and care about them as people?

7. How often do you have lunch or take a coffee break with some of your associates with no agenda other than spending some informal time together?

8. How often do you provide feedback to each of your direct reports over the course of a week? Do you praise each of your direct reports at least once a week? Do you nip problems in the bud by delivering corrective feedback immediately, in private, and in a respectful way? Are you always looking for opportunities to provide coaching that will help someone do their job better, even though their current level of performance meets minimum standards?

NOTES

1. Please pardon the sexism implied in this example, but my father was a man of his generation. He worked on FDR's Civilian Construction Corps and went on to serve in World War II. As I am sure you can imagine, he worked and my mother stayed home and took care of the house and family.

2. Fabior Sala, "It's Lonely at the Top: Executives' Emotional Intelligence Self [Mis]Perceptions," Consortium for Research on Emotional Intelligence in Organizations (2001). eiconsortium .org

CHAPTER 6

IMPROVING YOUR
DESCRIPTIVE SKILLS

IN WRITING THIS BOOK, I am making the assumption that you already have performance agreements in place with each of your direct reports. Performance appraisals typically end by establishing performance goals and objectives for the coming year. These must be written so that the goals and objectives are observable and measurable. Levels of authority should also be included in defining expectations. Nothing is more frustrating than to be held accountable for an objective but lack the authority to make it happen. Both you and the employee should be able to review the performance goals from time to time and agree on whether the employee is living up to your expectations.

Performance agreements should be reviewed and renegotiated if your expectations of the employee change over the course of the year. This is not unusual. Changes in the organization's structure of goals can result in changes in what is required of you and your staff. This should result in immediate group and individual meetings to clarify what is now expected of the group and each member of the team.

GOOD COACHING MAKES PERFORMANCE APPRAISALS EASIER

I can't recall ever meeting a manager who described doing performance appraisals as one of his favorite management responsibilities. Most leaders do performance appraisals because the organization requires them to and because Human Resources has systems in place to make sure they get done.

Performance appraisals become particularly uncomfortable for both people involved when there has been too little ongoing coaching throughout the performance year. If you use the coaching tools you'll study in this text, you will be in a position to do appraisals that contain absolutely no surprises for the employees involved. You will know that you are doing a good job as a coach when performance appraisals summarize all the coaching conversations you've had with the employee throughout the performance cycle. Then you can complete the appraisal interview by setting goals and performance objectives for the next review period.

If possible, ask your employees to do a self-appraisal and bring it to the meeting. This is one way to find out whether they have been listening to your coaching and whether they have understood you. If they end up with different interpretations of your coaching, you can be sure of one thing: You haven't done a good enough job of making certain that they understand you. Either you have been unclear or they are distorting what they think they've heard you say.

Now let's move on to the heart of the coaching relationship: all the conversations you have with people about their performance between formal appraisals. Do this job well and performance appraisals will be easy.

DESCRIBING PERFORMANCE: ELEMENTAL SKILLS FOR COACHING

Good coaches are experts at describing performance. This may strike you as so obvious as not to be worth mentioning. But it is not as easy as it sounds.

Try an experiment. Get out a piece of paper and list two examples of performance you've observed on your team recently. One example is something you observed that pleased you. The other is something that either was completely unacceptable or was acceptable but could still be improved. For our purposes in this book, these examples should involve aspects of emotional intelligence. For instance, the performance could be about translating the team's vision and guiding principles into action or about how the person interacts with individuals or groups in a way that either works well or doesn't work at all. Don't proceed until you have described your examples on paper.

Observing and Describing Performance

As a coach, you observe what people do, that is, you observe behaviors. You observe how well they are turning your company's mission and values into action. You also observe how well they are meeting your expectations of them, given their performance objectives and the directions you have provided from time to time. You see examples of the display of emotional intelligence—or the lack of it.

There are times when you don't have direct observations of your own. You don't look over peoples' shoulders all day long but you are able to observe the results they produce. Are their results produced on time and as specified? Another source of information is what you hear about them from others: their peers, other managers, their own direct reports, and their internal or external customers.

Over time, you develop a history of their performance based on various kinds of information: direct observations of their interactions with you and with others, the quality and timeliness of the results they have produced, and the comments and observations of others. Our brain is designed to organize information by sorting data into clusters that have an underlying organizing principle of some kind. The longer you manage someone, the more data you collect, and more of these conceptual clusters take form.

How you sort information into clusters is affected by your own values, expectations, assumptions, beliefs about people, and a host of other subtle organizing factors that influence your perception of the world around you, sometimes in ways that are below your conscious awareness. As you assemble clusters of data about your direct reports, the brain's next step is to make a judgment and apply a label to describe each cluster.

Without sorting, organizing, and labeling, the sheer volume of life experiences and observations would be overwhelmingly complicated. To make life easier and simpler to deal with, the brain assigns labels to these subsets of observations. We'll look at one cluster of behaviors, results, and observations shared from other people and label this cluster "professional." Another cluster we might label "proactive." Yet another gets interpreted as "highly productive and reliable."

We do the same thing with clusters that are not as positive. Your brain, using your values, expectations, and a variety of other variables, labels some information clusters with words like "bad attitude," "resistant to change," "passive-aggressive," or "hostile."

How Ambiguous Descriptions
Undermine Coaching

Having labeled a cluster, whether positive or negative, leaders with the best of intentions call someone in their office and say something like, "Tom, I really liked your presentation in the meeting this morning. Very professional." Talking to someone else, they might say something like, "I thought your response to Marie in the staff meeting was quite rude. I want you to be more polite from now on."

Note that in both situations the manager's intentions are good. The first example involved praise for a job well done. The other addressed the need for a correction in someone's behavior during staff meetings. Unfortunately, both examples use words that *sound* meaningful but provide nothing in the way of useful information. The person who was praised might feel good but doesn't understand exactly what the boss meant by "professional." The person who was told he was rude may have had no intention of being rude and, being a poor observer of himself, ends up with no idea of what specific behavior needs to be corrected or how to act more appropriately in the future.

Years ago I was a fan of *Mary Tyler Moore,* a sitcom set in a Minneapolis TV newsroom studio. In one episode, Mary was having problems with Ted, the bumbling, clueless anchorman. She went and complained to her boss, Lou. He responded, "No problem, Mary. I'll handle it." He called Ted into his office and said "Ted. You know the way you always are?" Ted grinned and straightened his tie. Lou then said, "Don't *be* that way."

I laughed and immediately copied down the lines to use as an example when training leaders in coaching skills. But surely, I thought, this wouldn't happen in the real world.

About a month later I was doing a consulting assessment of the management team of an engineering firm. I was interviewing one of the vice presidents, whom we'll call Tom. He said, "I'm not sure what is going on but the president is really unhappy with me." I asked him to elaborate. He responded, "The other day, he called me into his office and said, 'Tom, I don't know what it is you're doing, but every time I am around you I get irritated. I want you to stop doing that.'" Tom found that he was now all but paralyzed when in the presence of the president. He said, "I don't know what 'it' is but every time I'm around him, I'm wondering if I'm doing 'it' again."

I had come to know this president quite well in the early stages of establishing our mutual goals for the consulting project. He was an extremely shy man, a brilliant engineer, but someone who was very uncomfortable dealing with anything unpleasant or too personal in a conversation. I knew that the feedback he gave Tom was an act of courage. It wasn't easy for him to deliver corrective feedback. He had good intentions but unfortunately his feedback was as global and meaningless as "Don't *be* that way."

Descriptive Skills: From Labels to Specifics

Language is the tool used in coaching. The first step in becoming an effective coach is learning how to describe your observations and your expectations so clearly that there is little room for your associates to be confused or leave the conversation misunderstanding what you were saying to them.

The above examples of coaching were utterly useless. "Professionalism" and "rudeness" do have meaning, but a coach's job is to provide specific examples so there is no doubt about what you are talking about. When praising people, let them know exactly what you like so they know what to keep doing in the future. When providing corrective feedback, you have two descriptive challenges: describing *what* needs correction and *how* you expect them to correct it.

Consider our two examples of feedback, addressing someone who was "professional" in a presentation and the person who was "rude" during a staff meeting. Remember how your brain wants to simplify things by organizing clusters of data and slapping labels on them. Rudeness exists. So does professionalism.

Imagine a baseball coach standing behind the batting cage, saying, "You keep missing the ball. I want you to hit it from now on." This is not coaching. A good batting coach describes exactly what the batter is doing wrong and how to correct it. The coach may say things like, "Your left foot is too close to home plate. I want you to open your stance by moving your left foot out just a bit. You are only using your arms to swing and not getting enough power behind the bat with your wrists."

Telling someone they were "rude" and that they need to be "more polite" is about as useful as telling a batter he missed the ball and that he should hit it from now on. Coaching must include detail in order to be useful. Early in this chapter I asked you to write down two examples of behaviors you observed recently, one that you liked and one that needs improvement or correction. Are your examples specific enough to understand or are they global and nonspecific labels, leaving room for your associates to misunderstand what you meant to say?

DESCRIBING PERFORMANCE IN
NEED OF IMPROVEMENT

When you provide corrective feedback, you must describe what aspect of performance was either below standards or could be improved. You must also provide a clear description of what the person needs to do to improve. "Don't *be* that way" is not good enough.

Getting to specifics is not as simple as it might seem. In management training events, I have to do a great deal of coaching to get participants to be as specific and concrete in their language as they need to be. This takes practice. You'll find exercises in the Skill Development section at the end of this chapter. Please do them. The time you invest will be more than worth it when you start applying the coaching model presented in Chapter 7.

Look at the following list of examples. Each label is followed by an example of a more descriptive example a coach might want to address. But each label could be followed up by any number of different but equally specific examples. As you look at each example, pause for a moment and think about your own associates. If you were to coach someone about these areas of performance, what spe-

cific examples might you use to describe the performance of someone who reports to you?

Rude:
"You interrupted a coworker as she was making a suggestion
and told her that she didn't know what she was talking
about. You used a loud, angry tone of voice and your facial
expression conveyed the impression that you thought she
was stupid and clueless."

Unreliable:
"Over the past three weeks I have given you six different
assignments to complete by a specific time. You missed the
deadline on three of them and you failed to provide all the
information I requested on two of the projects, forcing me
to send you back with more instructions to complete the task
fully."

Negative Attitude:
"In the staff meeting this morning I noticed that you reacted
to the new documentation requirements by sighing and rolling your eyes. Then you looked at the person next to you
with an expression on your face that seemed to be saying,
'Can you believe what management came up with this time?'
On the way out of the meeting, I overheard you complaining
to your coworkers that this was 'another example of management creating needless paperwork.'"

Not a Team Player:
"On several occasions recently I have called for volunteers
to work on different projects. You never once raised your
hand to take on the extra work that has to get done. In addition, several people have told me that whenever they ask you
for extra help, you sigh and look irritated. You help out but

you act like you have been imposed on and that you don't like it, making the experience of working with you very unpleasant."

Needs to Be More Proactive:
"On several occasions recently, you have missed opportunities to better serve our customers by waiting for them to call you rather than making a call yourself to find out how they are doing and if there is anything you can do to help them out. I've also noticed that failing to call your customers puts you in the position of not having inventory on hand when they call you, forcing them to wait a day or two before you can provide them with what they are requesting."

Not Productive Enough:
"Developing new code for these kinds of features normally takes someone with your experience about two weeks. So far each of the features I've had you develop has taken three of more weeks from the time you start until you turn it over to product testing."

DESCRIBING PERFORMANCE THAT MEETS YOUR EXPECTATIONS

Describing good to outstanding levels of performance is a skill that also requires you to be as clear and specific as possible. Using the format that will be presented in Chapter 7, you will discover how to formulate and deliver effective praise in 15 to 20 seconds. As you'll see, clearly describing what you liked about people's performance is a critical step so that the people hearing the praise know exactly what they did that earned your recognition.

Here are a few examples of descriptions of good performance.

Once again, we'll start with a label of a cluster of behaviors. As you read the example, think about how this same label might be described more specifically, given your profession and the kind of work done by the people you coach.

Good Job with That Upset Customer:

"Even though she was angry, you listened to her without looking defensive and assured her that you wanted to take care of the problem. You also told her that you were sorry that she had to experience any inconvenience. Then you quickly resolved the problem."

Very Professional Presentation in the Meeting:

"Your presentation was well organized and easy to follow. You developed each idea in a logical sequence that made it easy for this group to understand, especially with the graphics that illustrated your data for each point. You looked very comfortable in front of the group and spoke very clearly and authoritatively.

Good Participation in the Staff Meeting:

"When Marie made her presentation in the staff meeting, you restated her major argument very clearly to assure her that you understood what she was saying. You were careful to acknowledge the work she had put into thinking through the problem. Then you offered another approach in a way that built upon the work she had done. I also noticed that your tone of voice was very friendly and supportive of Marie and her team."

Good Team Player:

"When Mark called for volunteers to work on his project, you volunteered and encouraged others on the team to give him a hand. I've also noticed that you have been very helpful to new employees and are always willing to spend time explaining parts of the job they are having difficulty understanding."

Inspiring:

"In discussing the importance of the work we do, you stress our clinic's commitment to making our clients' lives healthier and filled with more vitality. I've overheard you giving instructions to your staff and referring to our team's mission statement by including examples of how they make a difference in the quality of our patients' lives. Stressing that when people feel better they have better relationships with family and friends is also a way of letting your staff know that their work has a ripple effect that is much broader than simply taking care of a particular health problem."

You Do Good Work:

"Every assignment I've given you this week was done on time and needed no rework or corrections of any kind. I've also noticed that your documentation notes are very thorough, clearly written, and that anyone else who has to work on this project will have a good understanding of the work you've done on it."

Good Attitude:

"I've noticed that you add a great deal of energy to this team. You always seem to be in a good mood, you smile at people, and you never complain during crunch time when we have to close the books at the end of the month. Your attitude is infectious and I don't think the team would be the same without your spark, your optimism, and the 'can-do' approach to your work."

Skill Development

Before moving on to Chapter 7, do the following exercises in writing:

1. List the name of each person you are responsible for coaching. For each person, list one example of something they have done recently that either met or exceeded your expectations. Also list one example of something that each person did that either failed to meet your expectations or, while acceptable, could be improved by doing something a little differently.

2. Write a description of each of these examples, with the goal of being as clear and specific as possible.

3. Approach one of your peers and ask for a few minutes of her time. Explain that you are working on developing your coaching skills, and that right now you are developing your ability to describe performance so clearly that there would be little misunderstanding of what you are saying when you provide coaching.

Then read her the example you've written for each of your employees and ask your peer to paraphrase what she understands you to be saying. If you have to keep clarifying what you meant because she isn't able to paraphrase you accurately, you have more work to do on descriptions that are based on specific behaviors or results. If so, don't be discouraged. Describing performance clearly is a challenge. It is so easy to slip into the broader labels in spite of your efforts to describe specific behaviors or results. Keep practicing.

CHAPTER 7

SO NOW WHAT DO YOU SAY?

A Structured Format for Coaching

MANY MANAGERS AVOID OR DELAY COACHING because they don't know what to say when addressing someone's performance, especially when the performance is in need of correction. Awkward or overly harsh coaching results in a predictably defensive response by the person on the receiving end. Or the individual may accept the correction but if the coaching has been perceived as a personal attack, the relationship between the manager and the associate has been damaged.

Managers who are uncomfortable with coaching often approach a topic so carefully that their coaching is vague, tentative, and almost apologetic. Hesitant coaching lacks power and, in the end, erodes the credibility of the coach.

Conversations with thousands of employees and managers have led me to one firm conclusion: Almost every leader, from presidents to first-line supervisors, could do a better job of coaching than they are doing currently. Their coaching needs to improve in two ways. First, most leaders would benefit from mastering a structured format that makes coaching easy to formulate and deliver. Second, most leaders need to be far more active as coaches and need to make conversations about performance a routine part of their day. The structure needs to be easy to use and allow coaching to take very little time.

You have more than enough to do every day. If you are going to coach more frequently, you need a structure that will help you make the best possible use of a brief conversation. Coaching needs to be something you can easily squeeze into your already full day. For example, say you are on the way to a meeting and encounter some- one in the hallway, where a 30- to 60-second coaching interaction gets the job done. This allows both of you to proceed on your way with a minimum interruption in the flow of your work.

The following structure for coaching will allow you to have short conversations that make a big difference. Hundreds of leaders have used this structure with great success. So can you.

The format consists of four main elements:

1. Opening Statement
"I want to talk to you about *(the category of performance)*."

2. Observation
"I've observed *(describe the performance or behavior)*."

3. Impact
"The impact is *(describe the impact on the job being done)*."

4. Request
"From now on, I'd like you to *(describe how to improve per- formance/behavior)*."

Here is how each element works:

1. OPENING STATEMENT

"I want to talk to you about *(category of performance)*."

Every time you open a coaching conversation, you want to begin in exactly the same way. This is one way to help you manage the personal and professional relationships you have with your associates. You might have been having a short personal conversation. You may be talking about what each of you did over the weekend, about politics, or about a recent sports event. These kinds of conversations maintain your personal relationship with each of the people you manage.

Having a consistent opening statement to start a conversation about performance is a way of shifting the focus and tone of a conversation from personal to professional. In essence, you are saying, "Now I want to have a conversation with you as your boss." The opening statement in this structure is simple and straightforward. It lets the person know that you want to address some aspect of his performance, describes the category of performance, and makes him realize that it is time to listen carefully because he is about to receive feedback about his work.

Your opening statement will identify the general topic of the coaching. Obviously, the topics of coaching vary, depending on whether you are a supervisor coaching an associate or a senior-level executive coaching a middle manager.

Examples of performance categories for associates include:

The project you completed this morning

Your attendance record

Your punctuality at our team meetings

Your progress on developing a new feature for our software

The report you handed in this morning

Examples of performance categories for managers might include:

> The goals and objectives status report for your department
>
> The metrics you've collected on the quality of your team meetings
>
> Your annual budget report
>
> Some written comments we've received from your division's internal customers
>
> The plan you submitted for our reorganization

Other times your opening statement will address the expression of their emotional intelligence. Examples for associates might include:

> Your relationship with Jerry (a coworker)
>
> Your participation in the team meeting this morning
>
> Something I just overheard you say to a customer (or coworker)
>
> How you responded when Kathy disagreed with you at the staff meeting yesterday
>
> Something I noticed when my boss asked you a question in the all-staff meeting

Examples of topics related to emotional intelligence for managers and executives might include:

> How you led the team meeting I sat in on this morning
>
> Some information HR has gathered in exit interviews with people leaving your department
>
> Something I noticed about you when we were walking down the hall this morning

How you are living up to our company's value of listening to our associates

Metrics from your department regarding the frequency of coaching received by associates

Note that these opening statements are neutral in wording, that is, they just identify the topic you want to address. The purpose of this opening statement is to get your direct attention and put them into a listening mode.

2. OBSERVATION

"I've observed *(describe the performance or behavior).*"

Once you have their attention, you present them with a concrete and specific description of some aspect of their performance or an expression of their emotional intelligence. Your goal is to be so specific that there is little room for misunderstanding or distorting what you have said.

Memorize the structure as written. When you approach an associate or manager to provide coaching, the structure will help you organize your thoughts and deliver coaching in a sequence that thousands of managers have reported to have enhanced their personal comfort and effectiveness in providing coaching. You can even use the sentence stems as written but you want to develop your own natural style. You don't want your coaching to sound "canned" or like you've just been to a management seminar. So instead of saying, "I've observed . . ." you may open this part of the coaching sequence with one of the following:

"I noticed that you volunteered to help out on Jim's project this morning . . ."

"Your status report failed to include your targets for last Friday. . . ."

"I've received comments from some of your customers and they've reported . . ."

"I have some concerns about how you handled that disagreement in the staff meeting this morning. . . ."

You can formulate the observation step any number of ways, as long as it includes the specific description of something for which you want to praise someone or of the performance or behavior that needs to be improved.

3. IMPACT

"The impact is *(describe the impact on the job being done)*."

Although this sentence stem is probably the most stilted language in the entire structure, this section of the structure is of great importance. You are not bringing this topic up and investing time just to make idle conversation. You have described a specific aspect of performance or behavior. Now you want to make clear why you are bringing this to their attention: What they did or how they behaved had a positive or negative impact on the job in some way—customer service, costs, morale, the company's image, quality, efficiency, to name just a few. Another possibility is that the performance or behavior either lived up to or violated one of the team's guiding principles.

Describing the impact of what you've observed is a way of "professionalizing" the coaching conversation. When providing corrective coaching, you are not attacking this person's motives or character. Nor are you talking about your own feelings of anger or disappointment. This is a conversation about performance or behavior and how that is affecting the work being done by your direct report.

In discussing this section of the coaching sequence at a leadership development session, a manager in the back of the room murmured, "White socks." His comment made absolutely no sense to me but it evoked laughter from the group. When I asked what he meant, he said that he was always riding people about wearing white socks to work. But when he thought about how it affected their work, white socks made no difference at all. The manager recognized that this was a personal quirk of his and that he was going to have to give it up because white socks had no impact at all other than as a violation of his personal sartorial preferences.

Now suppose you manage someone whose job requires him to wear expensive dark blue or dark grey suits and dress shoes. His job brings him into contact with customer CEOs. He also makes occasional appearances on television, serving as a content expert on the industry in which your company is involved. It could then be argued that a $3,000 dark suit, expensive Italian shoes, and white socks were not a good combination. Given that person's role as the public face of the company, "white socks" would definitely have a negative impact on the polished professionalism the company wants to project.

Notice the role, then, of the impact statement. You will see how important this is when we look at corrective feedback regarding emotional intelligence. People often have personal habits or ways of communicating that undermine their credibility and effectiveness. When you start offering coaching on someone's habits that may be deeply personal in nature, you have to be able to demonstrate how this is affecting that person's performance on the job. That, after all, is the only reason you would bring the topic up for discussion.

4. REQUEST

"From now on, I'd like you to *(describe how to improve performance/ behavior)*."

What you have accomplished up to this point is a description of a behavior or performance and its impact on the job being done. Corrective coaching must also include suggestions on how to improve the performance or behavior. You have to be clear in your description of the desired level of performance, so clear that the receiver of corrective coaching will know exactly what to start doing differently from now on to make the necessary improvements.

Skill Development

Your assignment from this chapter is very simple. Write the entire coaching structure, including the sentence stems, down on a card or enter it into your PDA or Blackberry. Memorize the complete structure, word for word. Overlearning is useful. When under stress, we tend to fall back on old habits rather than use any new skills we have learned. Repeat the structure enough times so that you will be able to recall the entire structure any time you approach someone to provide coaching. The structure will help you organize your thoughts and make your communication more powerful and effective.

You'll find that the structure is so simple and logical that it won't take long for you to have it firmly implanted in your memory.

PART III

FROM THEORY TO PRACTICE: COACHING IN THE REAL WORLD

CHAPTER 8

PRAISE: SUCH A SMALL EFFORT—SUCH A HUGE RETURN

PRAISE. RECOGNITION FOR A JOB WELL DONE. A simple thank you.

I am sometimes asked this question: What is the single thing leaders could do that would make the greatest difference in performance and morale? The answer: To increase dramatically the amount of praise and recognition they offer the people who produce their products and serve their customers.

This would make a huge impact in so many ways. And it is so simple to do. You are about to discover that you can deliver effective praise in 15 to 20 seconds.

DELIVERING PRAISE

Praise serves as a reward and motivation for good work.

One of the most basic findings in psychology is that rewarding a behavior increases the likelihood that the behavior will be repeated. When people are doing something you like, recognize them for it.

Inspiring leaders are masters at providing recognition. They know that people want their efforts to be noticed and appreciated.

I once consulted to a small company with a staff of a little over 100 people. In my assessment interviews, I was told (over and over again) about the way the president of the company liked to end the week on Friday afternoon. He would wander around the company, approach people, and ask them what they did this week that they wanted him to thank them for.

This was so unusual that the first time it came up in an interview, I thought I had misunderstood what I was being told. I said, "Let me see if I understand what you're saying. He *asks* people what to thank them for and then he thanks them? And this actually works?"

Person after person I interviewed told me it was the perfect way to end the week. They had a moment with the boss and an opportunity to tell him something they had done that week that they were proud of but that the boss wasn't necessarily aware of. But what made it work was that the president was so genuine in expressing his appreciation. People would point out working late on a project for a customer or going out of their way to make certain a product got delivered on time, and the president would thank them with the kind of personal warmth and sincerity that made this unusual practice work very effectively. This practice had become so important to the employees that they missed it when the president was gone on a given Friday.

Praise Strengthens Your Relationships with Your Direct Reports

Remember that if you want to be effective at coaching for emotional intelligence, you must first establish trust and credibility. People must know that you care about them enough to pay attention to what they do. They also want to know that you genuinely appreciate their contributions to the work being accomplished by the team you lead.

Note the word, "genuinely." You have to mean it or praise doesn't ring true. In one project I was told of a hospital superintendent who used to tour the hospital every Tuesday morning. As he would parade through the different departments, he would be making comments like, "Hi, Daniel. Good to have you on the team" or "Hi, Mary. You're doing a good job." I asked people how they felt about this and they just rolled their eyes and laughed about him. They knew that the superintendent was "doing his leadership thing" as scheduled but it really didn't mean anything. His praise was so global and ritualistic that the practice became a joke among the staff. "Oh, good. It's Tuesday. Time to be told I'm doing a good job. I just can't wait."

Praise has to be specific to be effective. But it is even more important that you are expressing genuine feelings of appreciation. This is one aspect of your own emotional intelligence and personal values that deserves examination. You must truly care about people for your praise to be effective. Otherwise, your praise can be seen as manipulative or merely laughable, like that of the hospital superintendent.

Praise Paves the Way for Corrective Coaching

If you establish a practice of praising people frequently, they will be more receptive to your corrective feedback. And I am not talking softening corrective feedback with praise. If you start every corrective coaching conversation with praise, what does praise become? A signal that people are about to get yelled at or criticized in some way. "She's saying something nice to me. What did I do now?"

One of the reasons that managers sandwich corrective feedback with praise is that they are uncomfortable saying anything critical or negative to people. Put the skills you'll learn in this book to use and you'll become much more comfortable with coaching. That means providing people with information that will help them improve as well as holding them accountable when they are not living up to your expectations. But these conversations are so much easier for everyone involved when your relationship includes ample expressions of heart-felt praise. When people know that you have their best interests at heart, they are naturally more open to hearing how they need to improve.

Praise and Corrective Coaching Keeps People on Track

Did you know that *Apollo 11* was continually veering off course all the way to the moon for the first lunar landing? A group of engineers kept tracking its progress and putting in the course corrections necessary to get the astronauts to the right place at the right time. In a sense, that is what coaching provides: a guidance function to enable people to achieve their best possible performance.

You would like to think everyone you hire has an internal guidance system already built in and programmed. All you would have to do is give people a task and stand back and get out of the way. In fact, most of the people you hire want nothing more than to do a good job. I believe people are internally motivated to do a good job and that if they are not, no amount of coaching will make much difference. As a coach, you work with that already present drive to perform well, letting people know what they are doing well and when they need to make course correction, and doing so early enough for the information to make a difference.

I'll never forget a leadership development seminar I led for a county government early in my career. I had presented an analogy for them to consider—that coaching is a little bit like guiding someone who is blindfolded and put behind the wheel of a car. The only way the driver will arrive at the destination safely is by receiving corrective feedback—lots of it. To make the analogy more germane to management, you have to further imagine that you are in the passenger seat next to the blindfolded driver. And the road has a ditch on each side.

You can easily imagine how active you'd be in providing the driver with information in this situation. "Right. More right. No. Not that far, go left. A little more left." You can also picture yourself saying things like, "That's good. Keep going straight. You are doing just fine. Keep going. Oops, a little more to the left. That's good. You're right on track." It is the mix of praise as well as corrective feedback that will keep the car out of the ditch.

After my presentation, the county jailer raised a loud objection. First, you have to picture this guy. Well over six feet tall. Probably weighed in at about 250 pounds, most of it muscle. Came to the first session wearing his uniform and a gun. "What do you mean? I'm supposed to praise people for doing what they're being paid to do?" My first thought was, "Do I really want to argue with a guy this big who is wearing a gun?" My answer was, "Yes. Because it works. Praise lets people know that they are doing good work and that their boss is taking notice of it and appreciates it."

He came back to the second session and raised his hand to talk. "Let me tell you what I did. I went back to the jail and told people that I hadn't been praising them enough. I'd always assumed they knew that they were doing a good job as long as I wasn't chewing them out. So I said I was going to try praise out for a while to see what happens." Then he went on to describe two things that happened in the ten days between the two sessions. He noticed that praise had an immediate impact on morale. That is important, especially when working in an environment like a large urban jail. In addition, he was surprised at how much more work got done. Praise energized his staff.

Do you truly appreciate the efforts of the people who make it possible for you to be successful? Do you believe that verbal recognition from you is an important factor in creating a satisfying work environment for your team? For me to know the real answer to these questions, I would have to watch what you do. When it comes to coaching, action speaks louder than words.

WHY DON'T MANAGERS PRAISE MORE?

I have pondered this question for my entire career. Since 1980, in training rooms and consulting sessions, people have complained about the lack of recognition. As one person put it, "Would it kill my boss to say 'Thank you' once in a while?"

Dr. Gerald Graham surveyed 1,500 people from a wide variety of organizations and professions. As a leader in your organization, you should find his results to be both disturbing and a poke in the ribs to motivate you to become much more active in recognizing performance. His survey found:

- 58 percent of the respondents seldom if ever received personal thanks from their manager.

- 76 percent seldom if ever received written thanks from their manager.

- 78 percent seldom if ever got a promotion based on performance.

- 81 percent seldom if ever received public praise.

- 92 percent seldom if ever participated in a meeting designed to build morale.[1]

What is so disturbing about these findings is that Dr. Graham also asked people to rank order a list of sixty-five potential incentives available to managers to motivate and reward performance. The items listed above are, in rank order, the items identified as the top five most motivating strategies available to managers! Notice that three of the top five are simple activities that would take very little effort or time on the managers' part: personal thanks, written thanks, and praising someone in public.

I'll point this out just in case you missed it. The top-ranked item is an activity that takes about 15 to 20 seconds of your time to do effectively: offering someone personal recognition for work well done. A full 63 percent of the respondents rated a pat on the back from their manager as a meaningful incentive.

A recent poll done in Canada shows that things haven't changed much. Of 2,331 respondents to the poll, 27 percent reported that they had *never* received a compliment from their boss. Let me repeat that word: "never." Another 10 percent reported that they received their last compliment over a year ago.[2]

The paucity of praise is even more astounding given Buckingham and Coffman's findings that *weekly* praise is one of twelve essential management practices shown to be related to productivity, profitability, customer satisfaction, and employee retention.[3]

So why don't leaders make praise, recognition, and the courtesy of a simple "Thank you" the hallmark of their leadership activities? Most leaders agree that praise is important, that it leads to better morale, higher productivity, and builds a stronger relationship between leaders and their teams.

If most leaders agree that praise is so powerful, why is it that so many people complain of a lack of recognition at work? I think there are several factors at work here:

• Most leaders have good intentions but have so much work to do that praise falls to the bottom of the to-do list. Are you going to take time out to praise people when you arrive at work and discover that your desk is on fire? Put out one fire and another starts somewhere else and the next thing you know, it is time to go home.

• Most of the time, failure to meet standards is what gets attention. When was the last time a cop pulled you over and thanked you for using your turn signal and driving at the proper speed?

• The tone of the management team is set from the very top. Most CEOs and upper executives I've known are driven by their own internal standards. They don't feel a need for praise. They are focused on results. Since they don't need praise, they don't praise their direct reports. By failing to do so, they fail to establish the expectation that praise should become the norm in their organizations. In fact, in discussing this topic, many managers say that one reason they don't praise their people is that they never get praise from their own boss.

•   Finally, most of us are just not in the habit of letting people know how much we appreciate them, in our personal lives as well as our professional lives. At many funerals people are allowed to talk about the person who is the guest of honor. Many wonderful, touching, and funny stories are then shared. But I always wonder why we wait until someone dies to put all those nice things into words.

GUIDELINES FOR EFFECTIVE PRAISE

1. *Be genuinely appreciative.* If you are not genuinely appreciative of the work your people do every day, you'd better take another look. Every person on your team is doing part of your job for you. You are accountable to your boss for what they do. While it is important to acknowledge outstanding performance when it happens, most of what you see every day is being done by people committed to doing a good job and doing just that. You'd better appreciate the work they do. You depend on them to make you successful.

2. *Deliver praise from the heart.* Your appreciation of their efforts must be evident in your facial expression, tone of voice, and how you phrase recognition. You want them to feel that the work they do every day is important to you, to your department, to your company, and to your customers. If you are uncomfortable delivering praise, practice with a coworker, friend, or spouse until you can deliver praise with genuine warmth, connecting heart to heart with people who might, up until now, have heard too little from you.

3. *Deliver praise as soon as possible.* Don't wait until performance appraisal time to mention something someone did months ago. Coaching is a method of continually observing and shaping your

team's performance. When you see people do something that you can thank them for, do so immediately. Let them know that you noticed and that you appreciate them.

Genuine praise leaves people feeling good about themselves. People want to do work that is important and be acknowledged for their contributions. Praise will also make them feel better about you as their boss.

Finally, making comments about what you like to see makes it more likely that you will see those behaviors repeated in the future.

4. *Make praise specific and describe why you appreciate what people did.* Vaguely stated praise can sound insincere on the receiving end. It can even come across as manipulative. "Nice work on that report, Jim." Even if delivered with warmth and sincerity, this kind of global praise doesn't convey any information about what you liked in the report. By describing specific examples of what you appreciated, you assure your direct reports that you are, in fact, paying close attention to what they do.

5. *Deliver praise frequently.* Set a goal of acknowledging every member of your team at least one a week. Try this: On your calendar or some other place where you'll see it every day, write down the names of the people on your team. Did you observe something you could thank them for doing? If so, write *yes* next to their name. Did you acknowledge them? Write *No* next to the *Yes*. Make sure to acknowledge them as soon as possible, then cross their name off the list. Next week, start all over again.

Why is this important? You may have very good intentions, but you also need a procedure that reminds you of the need to praise and that helps you make sure people hear something good from you each and every week.

6. *Announce your intentions to praise people more often.* If you start praising people and this represents a noticeable change in your normal way of relating to people, they may wonder what is going on. At a team meeting, or one-on-one, you can tell people that you've

come to the realization that their contributions day in and day out are essential to the company's success. You have always appreciated them for what they do but seldom put it into words. Promise them that you are going to let them know what you appreciate about their performance more often than you have in the past.

7. *Praise people in public.* Acknowledging people in public accomplishes two things. First, most employees feel very good about being acknowledged in front of their peers. In addition, public praise is one way of reminding people on your team what you want from them. You can acknowledge people in a staff meeting or in their work area. Public praise will only cause resentment if you praise just a limited number of people on the team. If they are all used to hearing praise from you on a regular basis, public praise won't cause a problem.

Public praise is especially effective when people do something that is noteworthy. For example, someone might have worked very hard to make certain that a shipment arrived on the customer's dock on time. Perhaps there had been a shortage of some kind and the person found supplies elsewhere. Or maybe the customer called late but asked for a quick turnaround to avoid causing a disruption in service to her company's customers. Your company may have a value promising world-class customer service. Praising people in public for extra efforts to serve customers drives home how important this value is to the success of the company.

8. *Don't allow people to shrug off praise.* Some people are embarrassed by praise and will respond to it by saying it was no big deal or that they were just doing their jobs. Or they might just look uncomfortable. When this happens, say something like, "I don't want you to minimize the importance of what you did. You left that customer feeling well taken care of by our company and that is one of our most important guiding principles. You made a real difference today and I want you to know how much I appreciate your efforts."

9. *Remember that praise will not result in complacency.* Some managers fear that praise will make people complacent. Quite to the

contrary. Praise, effectively formulated and delivered warmly, leaves people feeling good about themselves and about your relationship with them. Praise raises morale and leaves people wanting to work all the harder. And because your coaching will also include corrective feedback, praise is a way of letting people know that you notice and appreciate what they are doing right as well as offering corrective coaching when improvement is needed.

STRUCTURED FORMAT FOR PRAISE

I want to remind you of the structured format for coaching, discussed in Chapter 7. You can use the same structure for praise, with one change. You end it with something like "Keep up the good work." You are not asking for an improvement. This is undiluted praise with no corrective element in the coaching. The rest of the structure remains the same.

Structuring Praise

1. Opening Statement
"I want to talk to you about *(the category of performance)*."

2. Observation
"I've observed *(describe the performance or behavior)*."

3. Impact
"The impact is *(describe the impact on the job being done)*."

4. Request
"Keep up the good work."

PRAISE TO ACKNOWLEDGE PERFORMANCE

In the following scenarios, the examples of praise do not parrot the sentence stems. As in all coaching, you need to develop a style of delivering praise that is natural for your manner of speaking. But memorizing the structure will organize your thinking and remind you of all the elements you want to include to ensure that your praise is as powerful as possible.

The Written Report

Each week you get a report from your direct reports that summarizes an important aspect of your business. In this case, the report from your inventory manager, Daniel, covers inventory on hand and expected delivery of new parts. Your business has recently shifted from an inventory-based system of manufacturing to "just in time." This procedure requires your managers to stay on top of available inventory and to keep parts coming in "just in time" to avoid disruption of the manufacturing line.

You might say something like this: "Daniel, I want to talk to you about your daily parts-available report. In the past month since we shifted to 'just in time,' you've done a great job of keeping track of what is available and what is coming in the next day. Your reports are always on my desk on time and clearly written. You are doing an excellent job of letting me know what is happening and whether or not we might be facing a parts shortage that needs my immediate attention. Keep up the good work."

Notice several things about this example. It starts with the standard phrase: "I want to talk to you about *(category of performance)*." This phrasing does not sound stilted or awkward, and you can use it every time.

The rest of the example did not use the sentence stems but included a description of what Daniel did (delivered clearly written inventory updates on time every day) and the impact (lets you know if there is going to be a parts shortage that requires your immediate intervention). Then the communication ends with, "Keep up the good work." It could end other ways as well, such as: "I just wanted you to know how much I appreciated your efforts" or "You're doing a great job keeping me informed. Thanks for your hard work."

Senior Executive's Planning Document

You are the head of the IT division of a large manufacturing company. You have just completed and distributed a document containing the goals and objectives your own boss is holding you accountable for over the coming year. You have asked the members of your senior leadership team to review your document and submit their own plans for their units.

You call Marie into your office and say something like, "Marie, I want to talk to you about the yearly planning document you turned into me yesterday. You obviously studied my goals and objectives carefully. You turned in a plan in which every goal and objective for your department is linked to contributing to the accomplishment of my own goals and objectives. I want you to know that I appreciate your attention to dovetailing your goals with mine. Now I know that your department's goals and objectives are clearly linked to helping me achieved mine. You just demonstrated the quality of thinking I was looking for when I promoted you. Good work."

The All-Hands Meeting

Suppose you have just had an all-hands meeting to bring the entire division up to speed on changes being implemented in your systems and processes. You asked each of your directors to take responsibility for parts of the presentation. Michael had a particularly tough job to do. He needed to explain a change in documentation, one that would require more work, but one that is critical for assuring regulatory agencies that your business practices are in accord with federal requirements.

"Michael, I want to talk to you about your presentation in the all-staff meeting. I thought starting out with a joke about giving people just what they want, more paperwork, was a great way to start. You managed to pull it off and get a good laugh. Then you went on to explain what is required in our documentation and how 100 percent accuracy in this documentation is critical in keeping us on the good side of the federal regulators who are tracking this information. You ended by acknowledging that no one likes to do any more paperwork than is absolutely necessary but you went on to remind them of a company that paid a huge fine because their paperwork was inaccurate and incomplete. You did a good job of driving home the point that documentation is mandatory and that complete accuracy is very important. Good work."

PRAISE TO ACKNOWLEDGE EMOTIONAL INTELLIGENCE

Notice that the previous example includes elements of both praising for performance (the explanation of the documentation and how important it was to complete it accurately) and praising for emotional intelligence (how Michael softened the impact of the new requirement by starting with a joke and ending with the acknowledgment that no one likes new paperwork but that this requirement was essential in avoiding a huge fine). The example addressed both *what* was done well and *how* it was done well. The following scenarios illustrate how to praise someone for a job well done.

Raising a Difficult Issue for Discussion in a Meeting

Martha is a key manager on your team. She runs an area that is critical to the functioning of the entire unit. She is in a position to see problems developing while they can still be dealt with easily. But Martha, though technically very skilled, is a very shy person and hates to engage in a conversation that might prove to be uncomfortable. You have been coaching her on how important it is for her to speak up before little problems become much bigger ones.

You call her into your office after a staff meeting and say, "Martha, I want to talk to you about your participation in the staff meeting this morning. I am really proud of you. One of our guiding principles encourages people to speak up feely in meetings and I know this is hard for you. You pointed out an emerging problem in the reports we are getting from accounting and how information needs to be added to avoid discovering we are over budget before it is too late to do anything about it. The accounting manager wasn't happy to hear this but you stood your ground. I felt like standing up and applauding. Good for you."

Managing Anger in a Meeting

You have been coaching a director who had been responding to disagreements in all-staff meetings by getting angry, red in the face, and responding harshly. This had always put an end to any further discussion of issues the associates either didn't agree with or didn't fully understand.

After the latest meeting, you call Dennis aside and say something like, "I want to talk to you about how you responded to Jim's statement that the new quality control checks are unnecessary and a complete waste of time. I thought you did a remarkable job of restraining your temper, especially since you are the one who implemented the new requirement. Instead of getting angry, I saw you pause and take a deep breath. Then you asked Jim for more detail, with the assurance that you don't want to add unnecessary tasks in a department that you know is already stretching to meet their production goals. You listened and paraphrased his argument to make sure you understood him correctly. The invitation to meet with you privately to see if the two of you can simplify the process was a good move. Thanks for not losing your temper and shutting the discussion down."

The Visionary Leader

As the CEO of your company, you were invited to attend a meeting of the customer services unit to launch a new service being offered by your financial division. The company has recently launched a campaign promising "financial services with a human touch." Up to this time, financial consultants have only been available by phone from 8 to 5. But many of your customers are at work during those hours and a recent focus group found that people want to be able to reach someone to answer questions about financial planning in the evening hours.

After the meeting, you call the director of the customer services unit into your office and say, "Janis, I want to talk to you about how you made the announcement that customer contact hours are being expanded to 10 P.M. I like how you tied the longer hours to our company's vision and the promise of 'world class service that sets the standards for our industry.' Then you pointed out how customers want to reach financial advisors in the evening hours. In the discussion, it was clear that everyone on the team understands the importance being available to our customers in the evening. I liked your idea of getting a group together to devise a rotational schedule so that no one will have to spend any more time away from their families than is absolutely necessary. Good job. It was a tough sale but you got the job done."

Reflections

1. If you are like most managers I've met, you could increase the amount of praise, recognition, and simple thanks you offer to

your staff. If you know you need to praise more often than you do, what gets in your way?

2. If your team were to receive more praise from you, what impact would that have on their morale and productivity?

3. Praise is one way of letting people know that you pay attention to what they do. Why is that important in maintaining productivity?

4. Make a list of the people who come to work every day and consistently perform within the acceptable range of performance. When was the last time you praised or thanked each of these individuals?

5. Over the next few days, watch what these employees are doing for your company. For each person, make a list of things they have done right that you could thank them for. Most of these examples will fall in the mid-range of performance. For example, they come to meetings on time. Their work is completed on time. They take on extra assignments without complaint. They treat their fellow workers and your unit's internal or external customers with respect. In other words, they are doing what they are being paid to do. These are all accomplishments that could be acknowledged.

Skill Applications

Now comes the fun part of your assignment from this chapter. It is time to start praising people more often.

Some reminders: Use the standard opener, "I want to talk to you about . . . ," and describe behaviors or results and why you appreciated what they did. End with a simple thanks or whatever feels comfortable to you. Speak from the heart. Most people have a good nose for insincerity, so be sure you mean it. You also have to deliver praise in a way that ensures your genuine feelings of appreciation come through.

Watch what happens when you praise people. When you do this properly, you can almost see people swell with pride when you recognize them for doing a good job. That response alone ought to be enough to keep you praising people. It will make both of you feel good about yourselves.

NOTES

1. Dr. Graham is the R. P. Clinton Distinguished Professor of Management at Wichita State University. He graciously granted me permission to include the findings of studies done in the early 1990s. His findings verify what I started hearing from people in the early 1980s and continue to hear to this day.

2. Jeff Buckstein, Special to *The Globe and Mail*, Toronto, June 15, 2005.

3. Marcus Buckingham & Curt Coffman, *First, Break All The Rules* (New York: Simon & Schuster, 1999). I urge my clients to purchase this book with a promise: If they don't get their money's worth out of the first chapter alone, I'll buy the book from them and give it to someone who'll appreciate it. I've yet to do so.

CHAPTER 9

CORRECTIVE COACHING
FOR JOB PERFORMANCE

PRAISE TAKES ONLY 15 TO 20 SECONDS. Corrective coaching can take more time, depending on the circumstances. In this chapter, we are going to examine several different strategies for corrective coaching:

- Using the structured format to enforce standards and expectations.

- Using part of the structured format to start conversations about performance. These conversations are designed to explore how employees understand the issue and get them involved in coming up with approaches to resolve the problem.

- Using mixed coaching. These are situations in which a mixture of praise and corrective feedback is the appropriate strategy.

QUESTIONS OFTEN ASKED ABOUT
CORRECTIVE COACHING

Sometimes you expect one thing and you get something else. In managing people, part of your job is to hold them accountable for meeting their performance standards and for developing more appropriate expressions of emotional intelligence. These are rarely comfortable conversations, for you or for the people on the receiving end of the corrective coaching. Using the coaching structure will make you much more effective at delivering corrective coaching. Before we look at strategies for corrective coaching, lets first examine questions often posed in executive coaching or in leadership development seminars.

- *Should corrective coaching begin or end with praise?*

No. If you are actively giving people praise, acknowledging their contributions, and saying thanks on a weekly basis, they already know that you notice and appreciate what they do well. This creates a relationship in which corrective coaching is more likely to be received without defensiveness. Your frequent coaching, including regular comments on what they are doing right, is a demonstration of your commitment to their success.

Corrective coaching must be provided in the spirit of helping people constantly improve. That means a good deal of coaching addresses performance or behaviors that are in the acceptable range but can be improved. Form a pact with your staff in which you promise to work together to help them perform at their very best. This makes coaching a partnership rather than an interaction based on authority and negative consequences. It changes the focus of your relationships with people to a mutual commitment to excellence. You become their ally rather than just an authority figure enforcing standards.

- *Should praise and correction ever be given in the same conversation?*

Yes, when coaching new employees who are learning their jobs or when coaching people in learning new tasks. Learning requires encouragement. This means noting what they are doing well as well as what they need to keep working on to improve other aspects of the skill or role they are learning. At the beginning of the coaching, coaches should define their role as an ally in the other person's learning. "That means I'll be providing you with coaching to help you master this new skill (or new role) as quickly as possible. My job is to let you know what you are doing well so you know what to keep doing. I'll also be providing directions and suggestions on how you can continue to improve." In learning new tasks, if all people hear about is what they are doing wrong, they can become discouraged and wonder if they are doing anything right.

• *Should corrective coaching be given in private?*

In general, it is best to do corrective coaching in private. A public "chewing out" is embarrassing and can result in the leader being seen as a scary figure. This can lead to people being more wary of raising issues or bringing up problems for discussions in meetings. The last thing you want to do is to suppress collaborative problem solving by correcting people in front of their peers.

Sometimes, however, you want to make a point that a certain behavior will not be tolerated and publicly addressing the problem is a way of driving this home to the entire team. Suppose you have established the expectation that all team meetings will begin on time and everyone attending the meeting will be present when the meeting begins. When teams have a habit of starting meetings late, people never know for sure when to show up. They might look at the time and think, "It's nine o'clock. I don't really have to be there for another ten minutes because we always start late anyway."

Starting meetings late is expensive. Suppose you have a meeting attended by twelve people once a week. Imagine that six to eight of the people show up on time and have to wait ten minutes or longer for the meeting to begin because other people straggle in late. This is a costly habit to allow your team to develop. If eight highly paid people sit idly for ten to fifteen minutes, that is costing you a good deal of money and time that could have been used more productively. (Compute the average salary of the group and figure out how much it would cost in lost time if every weekly meeting were to start

10 minutes late. Ten minutes may not sound like much but over the course of a year it adds up to a considerable waste of time and money.) Allowing meetings to start late also sets a standard of sloppiness that should not be permitted.

Establish the expectation that all meetings start and end on time and are driven by a prepublished agenda. Suppose you start your meeting on time, and two people come in 10 minutes late. You might say something like, "This meeting starts at 9 A.M. It is now 9:10 and both of you have missed the opening segment of the meeting. I have already made some important announcements, and now I am going to have to invest my time and that of the people who were here on time by repeating them. Whether you meant to or not, showing up late at this meeting conveys the impression that you have no respect for other peoples' time. From now on, I expect everyone on this team to be here at 9 A.M. sharp. Our meetings will start on time, with or without you, and I don't want to have to embarrass you or anyone else by having to talk about this again."

By correcting people in front of their peers, you are making clear that you expect this standard to be met and that people will hear about it in public if they don't make it on time. Issues that might be appropriate for holding people accountable in a public setting include violation of safety procedures, sexist or racist humor, the use of inappropriate language, an exaggerated display of anger, among others. The guiding principle is this: Correct people in public *only* when you want to drive the point home to the entire team that certain behaviors will not be tolerated.

- *What if I get a half-hearted response to my coaching?*

Then the conversation isn't over yet. Trust your intuition. If you get the feeling that their commitment to making the requested change is less than 100 percent, then follow up on it. You might say something like, "I am just not certain that you understand what I am asking of you. What can I count on you to do from now on?" If people can't accurately restate what your expectations are, then you need to clarify them by adding more examples or information.

Suppose someone says, "I'll try" or "I'll do my best." Respond by saying, "I'm not asking you to do anything you can't do. Whenever I hear 'I'll try,' I'm left with the impression that I am not going see the change in performance (or behavior) I am asking for. I want to know if I can count on you making the change I've requested. Can I count on you to do what I've asked?"

- *Is corrective coaching a two-way conversation?*

Absolutely. You must be open to learning more about why people are not meeting your expectations. That is why corrective coaching often leads to a short conversation. There are four possibilities:

1. *Employees may not have clearly understood your expectations.* If this is the case, clarify what you are holding people accountable for. You may have been too vague in your instructions, in which case you need to work on being more specific in the future.

2. *Employees may not have the skills required.* Employees may be working very hard to do what is expected of them. But you may learn in the conversation that their skills aren't strong enough. They may need more intensive one-on-one coaching to master the skills or they may require more training to develop the capabilities required to do the job expected of them.

3. *Something is preventing employees from performing.* Employees may know what you want them to do and have the skills to do it. In corrective coaching, you might discover that some organizational factor is preventing them from doing the job as expected. Information or materials may be slow in coming from another department, in which case you need to solve this problem with the manager of that unit. Perhaps the work process is flawed, in which case you and the team need to look at how work is being organized and look for ways to get the job done more easily and efficiently.

4. *The employees may not want to do the job as described.* If employees know what to do, how to do it, and nothing is stopping them from doing it, then the corrective coaching takes on more of an edge. You are asking someone to do some task or to behave in a certain way. Are they willing to do what you are asking or not? With continued failure in meeting your expectations, the conversation takes on a more serious tone. We'll discuss how to handle continued failure to respond to coaching in Chapters 11 and 12.

FORMULATING CORRECTIVE COACHING

If you haven't yet committed the structured format for coaching to memory, I urge you to review it again now:

Structured Format for Coaching

1. Opening Statement
"I want to talk to you about *(category of performance)*."

2. Observation
"I've observed *(describe the performance or behavior)*."

3. Impact
"The impact is *(describe the impact on the job being done)*."

4. Request
"From now on, I'd like you to *(describe how to improve performance/behavior)*."

This format will be especially helpful to you in formulating corrective feedback. It will remind you what to observe and how to organize your communication when you coach. Giving corrective feedback is stressful, and the structure will help you get the job done effectively.

Earlier in the book, we discussed the importance of describing behaviors or results so clearly that there is little room for misunderstanding your coaching. In corrective coaching, specific descriptions are just as important when you are describing what you want people to do from now on. This can be a challenge when coaching for emotional intelligence. After describing something that makes people less effective, you must also describe how they can perform or behave differently to improve their mastery of emotional intelligence.

EXAMPLES OF CORRECTIVE COACHING FOR PERFORMANCE

The Missed Deadline

You have given Mark a project to do with a specific deadline. On the day that it is due, he comes to you to tell you he is behind schedule and needs several more days to complete it.

You respond by saying, "Mark, I want to talk to you about how to handle deadlines in the future. You've just told me your project won't be completed until next week. My boss was counting on me to make a presentation on the project in the management team meeting Monday morning. Now I am going to have to call her and tell her it isn't complete. That makes both of us look bad and is going to slow down the progress we have been making on expanding our on-line customer service capabilities. From now on, if you have a deadline, I want you to do everything you need to get the project done on time. If you think you are going to miss a deadline, come and inform me immediately. This will allow me to help you identify the source of the difficulty and, if necessary, find people to help you out to make sure you meet the due date."

Opening Up a Problem-Solving Conversation

Sometimes corrective coaching is very clearly directed at improving an individual's performance and holding them accountable for meeting your expectations. If someone is chronically late to work or takes long lunch breaks, then you must enforce the standards. If someone is displaying the need for coaching for emotional intelligence, then you can clearly address the problem and what you want the employee to do. For example, if an employee's loss of temper frequently disrupts meetings and the exchange of ideas, your coaching should include how you want her to behave from now on.

But on other occasions, you must approach corrective coaching from the perspective of discovery. What is at the root of the failure to perform? One of the accepted principles in the continuous quality improvement movement is that most performance problems are due to faults in the system rather than the individual employee. In complex issues, such as late and incorrect billings, you describe the problem and its impact but then open the conversation up for problem solving. How do the people involved understand the situation? Are there problems in the systems, processes, and procedures that must be addressed before individuals can perform as expected? If there is a systems problem, you can make all the demands you want on the employee but they will not be able to meet your standards until the larger organizational issues are resolved.

Failure to Deliver Expected Services to Internal Customers

You manage an IT division that provides IT support to the company's independent business units. You have been getting complaints about the quality of services being provided by a unit in your division that supports the customer service department. Your IT unit is supposed to manage all of customer service's financial affairs, including billing and collections. The department manager has been complaining of bills going out late and with an unacceptably high error rate in the charges.

Note that in this situation any number of factors might be causing the problem. The customer service department may not be submitting the bills correctly. Or perhaps the equipment they use to record the services rendered is not functioning properly. So use opening segments of the coaching structure to start a conversation to get to the bottom of the problem:

"Sally, I want to talk to you about complaints I've received from customer services. I'm being told that bills are going out late and that there are too many errors in the charges. Their customers are unhappy with them and the manager of the department is threatening to outsource their IT services, meaning that you and your unit will be out of work. Tell me what is going on and how you see this situation."

Note that this example started with the standard opener and described the problem (late and inaccurate billings) and the impact of the problem on the customer service department (customer complaints) and the potential impact on IT jobs (if IT services get outsourced). Note that the coaching did *not* include, "From now on, I want all bills out on time and all billing errors eliminated." You are dealing with someone at the director level who knows what is expected of her and wants to perform well.

Your job as a coach and as an executive is to find out what is causing the problem. Is the customer service department failing to provide accurate information on time? If not, why not? Is this a procedural or systems problem? Does customer services lack the equipment needed to track usage of service accurately? If customer services is part of the problem, this is going to require you to get involved in resolving the issues that are preventing your people to get the job done accurately.

You may discover that the problem is internal to the unit. Perhaps the employees handling the billing need more training on the software and the interface between the line of business and IT. Or the problem could be a specific employee who is not doing a good job, and the director has been avoiding dealing with the issue because she doesn't like conflict. In this case, you would have to coach her on how to deal with the employee: either bring him up to speed or move him out of the organization.

Skill Development

1. Observe your direct reports and note performance that either fails to live up to expectations or falls in the acceptable range but could be improved with coaching.

Take several observations and write examples of corrective coaching, using the coaching structure as a guide. Check your written work to make sure you have included clear descriptions of the performance that needs improvement as well as how they can go about improving it.

2. Practice giving praise out loud until you can deliver corrective coaching smoothly.

Skill Applications

Once you are comfortable with your delivery skills, start offering corrective coaching for real. Begin by coaching people whose performance is acceptable but could be improved with coaching. Then move on to coaching people who are not meeting your standards.

Practice both kinds of corrective coaching. When holding people accountable, you deliver feedback as described using the entire coaching structure. For more complex performance problems, use the method in which you describe the problem and its impact but then ask the employees about their view of the problem.

CHAPTER 10

CORRECTIVE COACHING

TO DEVELOP EMOTIONAL

INTELLIGENCE

COACHING TO DEVELOP EMOTIONAL INTELLIGENCE requires you
to address aspects of a person's behavior that are deeply personal.
You will be most successful in addressing these kinds of issues if you
have taken the following steps we have already addressed in this
book:

- You have become a student of emotional intelligence. You
  will have done readings on the subject and be working hard
  on developing your own emotional intelligence.

- You have invested time developing a personal connection
  with your direct reports. In doing so, you have done your
  best to express your own commitment to helping employees
  be successful in achieving their personal and professional
  goals.

- You have looked for opportunities to praise each of your
  direct reports every week.

- You respond quickly to performance problems, doing your best to nip problems in the bud before they become major issues.

- You also provide corrective coaching to help people continually improve their performance.

Once you have established this kind of relationship with your direct reports, you are ready to start coaching for emotional intelligence. If you are a newly appointed leader of your team, you do not have to wait until you have taken all the steps listed above before coaching for emotional intelligence. You do quickly want to start to build relationships that include personal connection, caring, frequent praise, and performance-based feedback. But if someone's performance on the job calls for coaching for emotional intelligence, do not hesitate to provide necessary coaching.

CORE BELIEFS

Trainers and executive coaches base their strategies on assumptions and beliefs that serve as the foundation of their work. Here are my own beliefs that form the basis for my approach to coaching for emotional intelligence:

- *Most people want to do a good job.*
We have an innate drive to contribute and perform well at work. Coaching appeals to that part in all of us that wants to live a full and productive life.

- *Emotional intelligence is influenced by early life experiences.*
Each and every one of us has a unique history of experience that has made us who we are today.

- *Our behavior is always consistent with our view of the world and our place in it.*

Our behavior is determined by how we have learned to cope with life, given the events, circumstances, and people that shaped our experience from childhood to this very day. Maladaptive behaviors persist because what we do always makes sense to us; otherwise we'd behave differently. Besides, what we do appears to work for us so we keep doing it. That is as true for your direct reports as it is for you.

- *Lack of self-awareness is the greatest barrier in developing emotional intelligence.*

If we could see in ourselves what others see in us, we would choose to behave differently in some areas of our life and work.

- *The initial goal in coaching for emotional intelligence is raising self-awareness.*

Coaching holds up a mirror, helping people see themselves more clearly. This includes understanding how their behavior affects others. Help people capitalize on their strengths and work on emerging developmental needs. Developing their emotional intelligence is a never-ending journey throughout the course of their lives and careers.

- *Coaching personal behaviors must be linked to increased professional effectiveness.*

Coaching for emotional effectiveness is not intended to serve as a form of therapy. The goal is to address behaviors known to make people more effective in their work. Rooted in self-awareness, emotional intelligence involves managing ourselves and focusing our emotional energy on doing our jobs well and working effectively getting things done through and with other people.

BEHAVIORS THAT REQUIRE COACHING

The following list of potential behaviors requiring coaching to develop emotional intelligence is organized using Lynn's model of emotional intelligence, as described in Chapter 1. Here are a few examples of behaviors that would require corrective coaching.

- *Mastery of Purpose and Vision*
    - Lacks inspiration: Never talks about the company's mission and values in explaining decisions, changes, or giving direction.
    - Lacks a coherent personal vision for leading a unit. Does not link unit goals to the company's mission and vision nor bring own vision to this aspect of leadership.
    - Lacks a compelling vision and goals to fuel initiative. Only takes action based on specific directions from the boss.
    - Displays lack of drive to achieve. Does not display sense of urgency or personal passion about projects.
- *Empathy*
    - Fails to listen to coworkers or customers. Is only interested in driving own agenda without discovering the needs, feelings, and goals of others.
    - Attempts to listen but when paraphrasing what others say, is completely off the mark.
    - Displays lack of caring about how events affect other people, including own staff.
    - Is unable to read organizational dynamics and makes suggestions or raises difficult issues at a time when others involved are least likely to be receptive.
- *Self-Awareness and Self-Control*
    - Behaves in ways that reveal a complete lack of self-confidence.
    - When angry, takes issues personally and lashes out in attacks on others' motives.

- When angry, withdraws from conversation but continues to look very upset and angry.

- Uses anger to overpower others and get one's way.

- Appears fearful and anxious. Reluctant to speak up in meetings.

- Is very shy and socially withdrawn and is unable to connect with others.

- *Social Expertness*

  - Displays lack of honesty and integrity. Says one thing but does another.

  - Is untrustworthy. Doesn't keep promises. Gossips about people, in violation of the team' guiding principle banning gossip.

  - Is inflexible in the face of change. Resists it. Tries to find ways to block it.

  - Fails to represent management's point of view in explaining change to own staff.

  - Does not reach out and connect with other people in the company.

  - Is self-absorbed. Only looks at issues from own point of view.

  - Is sarcastic and uses inappropriate use of humor.

  - Has "tics" or personal mannerisms that create a bad impression.

  - Fails to establish close relationships with direct reports.

  - Avoids contact with senior management.

- *Personal Influence*

  - Takes conflict very personally.

  - Avoids conflict and does not share own point of view in meetings, a failure to live up to the team's guiding principle encouraging free and open discussion.

- Fails to intervene in conflict on own team.
- Doesn't encourage cross-functional collaboration.
- Sets unclear goals for own staff.
- Fails to hold staff accountable. Allows problems to linger.
- Does not share information from management team meetings with staff.
- Does not raise issues to represent unit needs.
- Makes presentations without connecting with the audience or displaying enthusiasm for the topic.
- Raises issues poorly. Whines and doesn't present a compelling argument.

Notice that these are broad categories of performance. In coaching, you would have to provide much more specific, detailed behavioral descriptions.

FOUR STEPS IN COACHING FOR EMOTIONAL INTELLIGENCE

1. *Provide feedback to raise self-awareness.*

People displaying self-defeating behaviors are often unaware of their own ineptness. Assume they have good intentions but poor execution.

2. *Help people "own" the behavior.*

People will be unmotivated to change until they accept the fact that their current coping strategies are ineffective and producing unintended consequences.

3. *Help people formulate a change strategy to improve targeted behaviors.*

Be prepared to offer specific directions or suggestions but see if people can arrive at their own strategies to improve targeted behaviors.

   4. *Provide continuing support for change efforts.*

Continually observe people and provide coaching to support change efforts. This will often be mixed coaching, noting improvements and ways to continue making progress toward the goal. Follow-up coaching should be provided as quickly as possible after the original coaching conversation. Let people know that you are paying attention and are an active supporter of their personal change efforts.

SPONTANEOUS COACHING

Sometimes you will provide a complete coaching communication using the coaching structure. You do this when the behaviors being coached are relatively minor issues and easy for the other person to understand and accept.

   For example, suppose you just observed someone make a presentation at an all-staff meeting. You noticed that the presentation was very well prepared but that her voice was low, she made no eye contact with the audience, and she appeared to be nervous and lacking self-confidence in front of the group.

   This calls for mixed feedback. You call her aside and say: "I want to talk to you about your presentation in staff this morning. There were many things you did well, and I also have suggestions for improvement.

   "You were very well prepared. Your organization of the material was clear and logical. Your PowerPoint presentation supported your main points.

   "In front of the group, however, you appeared nervous and lacking in self-confidence. Your voice was low and monotone. You rarely made any eye contact with the audience. The next time you give a presentation, I would like you to do a practice presentation for me. I want to work with you on how to appear more confident by standing straight and making eye contact. We also need to work on your vocal volume and how to use changes in pace and volume to drive home your points more clearly.

Again, kudos for your preparation. Well done. All we have to do now is work on your presentation skills and you'll be so much more effective. I know you can do this."

More Extended Conversations

Coaching for emotional intelligence will often call for a more extended conversation. When you are dealing with behaviors that are very personal and may be hard for the person to accept that a change is needed, your coaching strategy should adjust to allow a little more time for the conversation.

Suppose you just held a staff meeting. When Sarah disagreed with Mike's proposal for offering a new service to customers, his face reddened and he responded very angrily. He attacked Sarah directly, accusing her of being too lazy to take on a little extra work and of never supporting any idea unless it is her own.

The purpose of the meeting was to come up with new customer service innovations. Mike's outburst put the kiss of death to the conversation. Mike is one of the most outspoken and aggressive people on the team and his fits of temper seemed to cow the rest of the group. You tried to pull other ideas from the group but people were reluctant to share, lest they become another target for Mike's anger. In frustration, you stopped the meeting and rescheduled it to continue in one week.

Coaching Strategy for an Extended Conversation

1. *Set a time to meet.*
Call Mike aside and tell him you would like to talk to him about

his participation in the meeting. You need about fifteen minutes of his time. Set an appointment for him to come to your office.

2. *Open with partial feedback.*

Start the coaching session by describing what you observed and what impact Mike's behavior had on the meeting. You might say something like:

"I want to talk to you about what happened in the staff meeting this morning. I am very concerned about your response to Sarah's disagreement with your proposal. You took her disagreement very personally and got extremely angry. Your face got red and you were almost yelling at her. You accused her of disagreeing because she is too lazy to take on the extra work your project would require of her team. You also accused her of never supporting any idea that wasn't her own. This was a personal attack on her character and motivation. This was clearly out of line with our guiding principle that we deal with disagreements professionally and treat each other with respect.

"Your outburst ended the meeting. I intended for us to come up with new customer service ideas but people stopped participating after your fit of temper. I think the group was afraid of raising an idea for fear that you would attack them. I finally had to stop wasting our time and reschedule the meeting."

3. *Determine whether the employee acknowledges that the behavior is a problem.*

Your goal at this point is to see how Mike views his behavior and whether or not he sees it as a problem. You might say something like: "Mike. Help me understand this. I'm sure you do not consciously intend to alienate people and shut down creative conversations. Do you see that your anger is inappropriate and is sabotaging your effectiveness on the team?"

Mike might begin by offering excuses. Suppose he says that he is just passionate about his work and doesn't think his behavior is a problem. Use "empathic assertion" in situations like this. "So you think you are just expressing your passion for your work and think that other people should be willing to take you on. At the same time, did you notice that your anger effectively put an end to the meeting? Do you see how your anger is becoming a problem that I cannot ignore because of the damage you are doing to your relationships and the effectiveness of our meetings?"

Mike may even be unaware of his impact on others. Through a long series of life experiences, he has learned that the only way to be heard is to overpower people. He has never learned that disagreement with an idea is not a personal attack on him. Other people may have opinions to express that will expand on his idea and make it more workable, if only he would have the self-control necessary to keep his anger in check.

Your goal is to get Mike to agree that his behavior was out of control and inappropriate. You want him to agree that his behavior has unintended negative consequences, in this case stopping further discussion and damaging his relationship with Sarah.

If Mike agrees that his behavior needs to be changed, then your conversation can proceed to problem solving. But suppose he maintains his position that he is only expressing his passion and if people can't stand the heat, they should get out of the kitchen. In this case, you would have to draw on your authority and demand a change, describe it clearly, and let Mike know that you want to see results. This example continues with an illustration of both possibilities.

4A. *Employee acknowledges that the behavior needs to be changed.*

If Mike acknowledges that his anger is a problem he needs to work on, get him involved in exploring what he might do to control himself in the future. For example, you might ask him what internal cues tell him that he is about to lose his temper. Does he feel his chest constrict? Can he feel his face getting warmer? Is he aware of rising feelings of anger and defensiveness? Does he have a pattern of thoughts that precede an outburst, such as "I'm not taking this kind of crap from anyone"?

The action plan should include identifying ways to catch himself in the act and get control of his emotions before it is too late. If Mike can recognize the internal cues that signal an outburst is about to occur, you can suggest that, every time he notices those cues, he should say to himself, "There I go again. I'm about to lose it and say something stupid. Okay, I need to take a deep breath and remind myself that this isn't personal. The other person has a point of view that deserves to be heard and I owe her that respect."

Any number of other strategies might be agreed upon at this point. For example, your company may offer an Employee Assistance Program in which Mike can get anger management training. He might agree that his anger has been a lifelong problem and that such a program might be appropriate. The company may offer internal coaching or training in conflict management that might help Mike. At the very least, you need to agree on a plan that will enable Mike to work on this pattern of behavior and express himself more appropriately.

4B. *Employee does not acknowledge that the behavior needs to be changed.*

In this case, you need to be prepared to put your foot down and insist on change. You might say something like, "Mike, I don't agree with your view of this situation. You are not just expressing passion. You are expressing anger, loudly and abusively. You even question the motives and competence of your fellow managers. I will no longer accept this kind of behavior from you.

"In the future, when someone disagrees with you in a meeting, I do not want you to get angry, yell, and overpower the person involved. Instead, I want you to take a deep breath to get yourself under control. Remind yourself that losing your temper is unacceptable. Try listening instead. Paraphrase what you think the other person is saying to make sure you are understanding them correctly and that anger isn't clouding your listening."

5. *Use follow-up coaching.*

Observe Mike carefully in future meetings and look for any

movement in the right direction. In changing complex, deep-seated behaviors, you may have to provide mixed feedback for a while, praising progress while offering corrective coaching to continue improving the behavior.

For example, after the next staff meeting, you might call Mike aside. In follow-up coaching, always refer back to the earlier conversation. "Mike, I want to follow up on the conversation we had about your anger in meetings. When Jim pointed out that your department has been slow in getting out your daily summary reports, I saw you visibly struggle to maintain control of yourself by taking a few deep breaths. Your face got red and you looked upset. But you did make a good attempt at paraphrasing Jim's point. I did notice your tone of voice was a bit sharp and revealed that you were upset but you did not explode the way you used to. Overall, this is the kind of improvement I want to see you keep working on."

In time you may be able to say something like, "Mike, I want to follow up on our conversation about your anger in meetings. I've noticed a significant change in you over the last three months and I am very pleased. You haven't yelled at anyone for a long time. You are doing a good job listening and paraphrasing the other person's point of view to make sure that you understand them clearly. You still get a little bit red in your face but you are managing not to look so angry. Your voice is much calmer and you are more receptive to disagreement.

"Have you noticed how much more freely the rest of the group speaks up since you started working on your anger? We're having better discussions now because people feel safe to make contributions. Keep up the good work. I am very pleased."

Skill Development

1. Observe your direct reports. Look for behaviors that suggest a need for improving emotional intelligence. Take several observa-

tions and write examples of corrective coaching, using the coaching structure as a guide. Check your written work to make sure you have included clear descriptions of the performance that needs improvement as well as how they can go about improving it.

2. Practice delivering coaching for emotional intelligence out loud until you can deliver it smoothly. You might ask a fellow manager to serve as a role-play partner and listen to your corrective coaching. Then ask her to paraphrase what you have said to make certain that you were clear.

Skill Applications

Once you are comfortable with your delivery skills, start coaching for emotional intelligence. Start by offering coaching on behaviors that are easier to tackle. Deliver spontaneous coaching and the more extended conversational coaching when the occasion calls for it.

Be patient with yourself. Write down notes to help you remember what you want to say. After each episode of coaching for emotional intelligence, review the conversation and ask yourself what went well and how you might do better next time. This is the most challenging coaching you'll ever take on as a leader. With practice, you'll only get better and more comfortable with these kinds of conversations.

CHAPTER 11

PREPARING FOR A FORMAL
COACHING INTERVIEW

UP TO NOW, the coaching strategies we've discussed have required little or no advanced preparation. Hopefully, informal coaching conversations will nip most problems in the bud. But when they don't, a more formal approach to coaching is appropriate. As you will see, this will require you to gather documentation, using a worksheet designed for that purpose. Then you will organize and transfer that information to another form designed to help you present an organized communication to the employee.

Chapter 12 will describe a structured format to keep this conversation on track and to make it clear to the employee that your patience with their lack of response to coaching is wearing thin. The forms and interview structure are all designed to bring more management authority into the conversation. You may even go so far as to forecast formal disciplinary action if the desired changes do not occur.

Most people have the technical skills required to perform well. When they don't, coaching in those skills will usually bring the person around. One study reported that 90 percent of terminations are due to attitudinal problems, inappropriate behaviors, and the inability to form effective interpersonal relationships.[1] When you are faced with needing to do a more formal coaching intervention because coaching up to that point has failed, this study suggests that 9 times out of 10, the topic to be addressed is some aspect of emotional intelligence.

GATHERING AND RECORDING INFORMATION

This formal coaching interview may be your final effort in helping the employee develop some aspect of her emotional intelligence. It is hard to tell why the coaching hasn't worked up to now. Perhaps you haven't been clear enough in describing the behavior and she still hasn't developed self-awareness. Or she may not agree that the behavior is as serious as you judge it to be. Finally, she may want to change but needs more detailed and supportive coaching in helping develop new behaviors. The first step in preparing for this interview is to gather information, observations, and examples for you to use during the discussion.

THE COACHING PREPARATION WORKSHEET

You may reproduce the Coaching Preparation Worksheet found at the end of this chapter, or download it from my website, bobwallonline.com. The purpose of this Worksheet is to gather information and examples. Observe the employee for several days, jotting down specific examples for your discussion. Don't worry about neatness. You will organize and transfer this information to a different form before the interview. You may also approach other managers who interact with the employee to gather their perceptions to help you be prepared with specific and concrete examples to bring into the conversation.

1. *What is the performance problem that concerns you?*

If the topic is some expression of emotional intelligence, you need as many concrete examples as you can gather. You are preparing for a conversation in which you want to make clear that your tolerance for the lack of an appropriate response to your coaching is over. You want to see change and you want this conversation to be the turning point.

It may be that you are dealing with an expression of emotional intelligence that is difficult for someone to see in himself. If so, you need to come to this conversation ready with several examples of the behaviors that concern you. Read your examples to a fellow manager and ask her to describe, in her own words, the behaviors that need to be improved. If she is unable to paraphrase your descriptions accurately, then you are not ready for the interview. You need to make your descriptions so concrete and specific that there will be little room for misunderstanding.

2. *What is the impact of the performance problem?*

You are going to the trouble of preparing for a formal coaching session for one reason only, which is that the performance problem has an impact you cannot continue to ignore. In coaching for emotional intelligence, you must persuade the employee that the behaviors affect their success on the job. For example, an employee may get frustrated and angry when other people don't immediately agree with him. Once his emotions get aroused, he loses his ability to state his case clearly. In addition, his anger alienates people and they begin to stop listening to him. In time, the employee gets a reputation for being quick tempered, resulting in even further damage to his reputation and his relationships at work.

In spite of an employee's technical abilities, maladaptive behaviors like these may very well represent the lid on his career. If he is

unable to get along well with others and deal with conflicts appropriately, he may not be considered for promotions to positions that
require more contact with people.

You want to be as persuasive as possible in the coaching interview. You want to be able to describe several ways in which the
employee's behavior has a negative impact on his career success.
Although you have coached him in the past, he hasn't gotten the
message. So you want to go into this conversation prepared to finally
get through to him and raise his self-awareness of a career-limiting
activity.

In addition to talking about the impact on his career, you also
want to discuss other ways in which the behavior affects the job your
team is getting done. For example, his behaviors may slow down
decision making or limit the creative discussions that happen in
meetings. Or he may be alienating people whose support is badly
needed for the unit to be successful. Any impact you can think of
should be noted in your preparation. You want to be in a position to
persuade the employee that the behavior is serious and that it must
be changed.

3. *What do you want to see the employee doing from now on?*

Perhaps one of the reasons your coaching has failed to resolve
the problem is that you are dealing with a complex behavior that is
not easy for the employee to change. So you must go into the formal
interview prepared to describe exactly what steps the employee can
take to resolve the problem. This should include identifying circumstances that trigger the behavior and ways of coping with the situation more effectively.

Suppose you are dealing with someone who withdraws into sul-
len silence whenever people disagree with her. Rather than staying
in the conversation, she stops contributing but makes it clear that
she is very unhappy. She looks upset, sighs, and at the end of the
meeting slams her notebook shut and stalks out of the room without
speaking to anyone.

Signs of internal tension almost always occur before someone loses control. One strategy is to help her identify these internal cues early enough so that she can catch herself in the act and make a choice to behave more appropriately.

For example, she may tell you that when she starts to get angry, her chest gets tight, her breathing pattern changes, and her face and ears start to feel warm. In addition, she may notice a pattern of thoughts, such as, "Why can't these people understand something that is so obvious? Are they stubborn or are they simply dense?" Once you help her identify the internal cues preceding the behavior, you need to help her come up with a coping strategy.

Suggest that the employee start identifying the internal cues in the heat of the moment. As soon as she notices them, she should say something to herself like, "There I go again. I'm starting to lose it. I need to take a deep breath and remind myself not to take this personally. Withdrawing used to work with my sisters but I'm an adult now. I need to state my case the best way I can but remember that no one gets their way all the time." In addition to helping her develop strategies to identify and gain control over her feelings, you need to suggest more adaptive ways of dealing with the situation.

In this case, suggest that she pause, make a conscious decision to control her frustration, and remind herself that angry silence will undermine her credibility and damage her relationships. She should make a conscious decision to remain calm, soften the expression on her face, and continue to make eye contact with people in the meeting rather than withdrawing and looking down at her notebook. In addition, she should ask herself if she has stated her case as persuasively as possible. If so, she has done everything she can.

Your coaching should also include the reminder that, at work, she won't always get her way. It is not personal. People can, in good faith, end up with very different opinions about a professional issue. Your employee must understand that you win some and you lose some. As long as she has responsibly stated her case, she has done the best that she can do. Getting angry and taking it personally won't help and will only damage her career, and so she needs to learn how to accept disappointments more gracefully.

4. *What will you do if you see no improvement?*

Is this problem so serious that you intend to initiate formal discipline if the employee doesn't respond appropriately to your formal coaching interview? If so, be sure to check with your Human Resources Department for guidance on documentation and appropriate next steps. Employees like this often have a record of good performance appraisals because no manager has coached them on these problem behaviors in the past. HR may have steps for you to consider, such as training or individual coaching by an internal or external consultant. They may also suggest referring an employee for a medical or psychiatric evaluation to see whether there is some underlying physical disorder or the need for medication and psychotherapy to correct unacceptable behavior in an otherwise valuable employee.

Discuss this situation with your own manager. Review what steps you have taken up to now and find out what recommendations your manager has for you, especially regarding next steps. You don't want to talk about imposing consequences until you know you have your manager's support before the conversation.

Other less severe consequences may be available to you without resorting to formal discipline. For example, you may tell her that further angry withdrawals will force you to remove her from involvement in high-profile projects that bring her into contact with people from other departments and with senior management. This will obviously have an impact on the visibility that is so important to her career development. You don't want to have to impose this consequence but you will be forced to if she doesn't gain control over her behavior.

Skill Application

Either download or make a copy of the Coaching Preparation Worksheet that is shown on the following pages. Pick an employee who needs corrective coaching and complete the Worksheet as if you are preparing for a formal coaching interview. If you have an employee who has not been responding to your coaching, use that employee as your example in working with the Worksheet. By the end of this book, you'll be ready to conduct a more formal coaching intervention. If you do not have anyone who requires this level of coaching right now, think about someone you may have had difficulty coaching in the past and use that person for your example in practicing working with the Worksheet.

NOTE

1. Marlene Lozada, "Social Misfits, Workplace Outcasts," *Vocational Education Journal* 71 (February 1996): 14.

THE COACHING PREPARATION WORKSHEET
(Confidential)

Name of Employee

1. What is the performance problem that concerns you?

(Describe the problem in terms of *behaviors* and/or *results*. What is the employee doing or not doing that concerns you? Describe several examples of the problem before you proceed. Be as specific and concrete as possible in describing behaviors if emotional intelligence is at the heart of the problem.)

2. What is the impact of the performance problem?

(Why does this concern you? What is the impact on the work done by your team? On your customer? On the quality of your service? Also include examples of the potential impact of the lack of change on the employee's career development.)

3. What do you want to see the employee doing from now on?

(What behaviors or results do you want to see from now on? You must be so clear in your description that the employee will know exactly what is expected from now on.)

4. What will you do next if you see no improvement?

(Is this conversation a "verbal warning"? If so, the next disciplinary step would probably be a written reprimand. If you are not taking a disciplinary approach at this point, are there any consequences you want to discuss if improvement is not satisfactory? For example, demotion from a management position to an employee role? Change to a different set of responsibilities?)

CHAPTER 12

STRUCTURING THE FORMAL
COACHING INTERVIEW

THE PURPOSE OF THIS INTERVIEW is to create a turning point in coaching with people who have not been responding to your more informal coaching efforts as you might have hoped. This is a more formal conversation in two ways:

1. You will have created written preparation to make sure you communicate as clearly as possible.

2. You will conduct a *structured* interview to make certain that you maintain control over the meeting, get your message across, and get a commitment from the employee to make the changes you have requested.

THE FORMAL COACHING INTERVIEW FORM

Either reproduce the Formal Coaching Interview Form found at the end of the chapter or download a copy of the Form from my website, bobwallonline.com.

This form will serve you in several ways:

- *The form will help you structure the Formal Coaching Interview.*

Organize the information you have gathered on the Coaching Preparation Worksheet (see Chapter 11) and record it on this form. You will use the completed form during the interview to make sure you communicate your views completely. The format of the form is very similar to the coaching structure first introduced in Chapter 7. One additional step has been added to the structure: What you will do next if the employee's behavior does not improve.

- *The form will serve as a record of the interview.*

Check with your HR representative regarding policies, union agreements, or state laws regarding documentation of efforts to coach people. This form can serve as your own private record of the conversation. At this point do not give a copy to the employee or put it in his personnel file, because doing so elevates the intervention to formal disciplinary action, something you are still trying to avoid. Should this coaching relationship deteriorate and end up in a grievance hearing or other legal action, you will be able to retrieve this form from your file and have a record of what you said on a certain date in a coaching session.

Note the form has a section titled *Summary*, which is to be completed after the meeting. After the employee leaves your office, make note of any significant response from the employee during the interview. If you are allowed to keep an informal, personal record such as this, do so with three cautions in mind:

1. *This is your personal information and is not to be given to anyone else.* If this is your own record of the interview, do not give a copy to the employee. If you get promoted, do not pass this form on to the manager who succeeds you, because

that would result in two personnel files. One is the official personnel file held by HR, and the other would be a secret informal file passed from manager to manager that is unavailable to the employee. This would be an infraction of labor practices in most states.

2. *You want to be able to read your own writing at a later date.* Should the situation deteriorate and lead to termination, make sure your written notes are legible enough that you will be able to read them at a later date. Some people use bullets. Others fill in the form in sentences using very neat, small print. Also be aware that your notes are open to subpoena in a legal action. Therefore, don't write anything in the Summary that would haunt you at a later time.

3. *Avoid giving a copy of the form to the employee.* Sometimes employees will ask about the form and request a copy. If this interview is your final effort to salvage the employee without getting into the formal disciplinary process, say something like, "This is just a form I used to prepare for the interview. Don't worry. It is not going in your personnel file."

If the employee persists in requesting a copy, say this:

"If I give you a copy of this form, that will elevate this conversation to formal discipline. I am trying to avoid doing that. I would be forced to put a copy of this form in your personnel file. Having it in your file would be a negative mark on your record if you were to be considered for promotion or a lateral transfer to a more challenging job.

"I don't want to do that to you. I'm hoping that you and I can once and for all resolve this problem and keep it out of the official records. I am committed to keeping this conversation informal if you are willing to work with me and make the changes I have been requesting."

FACTORS TO CONSIDER

Your Mindset Approaching the Interview

You may already be frustrated going into this meeting. You have been providing coaching to an employee, but he has failed to make the necessary changes. You have to remind yourself that your intention in this meeting is to make him more responsive to your coaching.

You want to conduct this meeting with a very serious approach. Not angry or punitive, but in a matter-of-fact and no-nonsense manner. In setting up the meeting, approach the employee and ask him if a certain time is open in his calendar for a meeting in your office. If he asks you what the meeting is about, just say that you want to have a talk with him and that you want to make sure that he has at least 45 minutes available to cover everything you want to talk about. In talking with him to set up the meeting, don't make small talk or jokes. Keep the conversation strictly professional.

Where to Conduct the Meeting

Conduct the meeting in your office. This is where you are most comfortable. Your office is also a symbol of your authority. When the employee arrives for the conversation, greet him, but again in a matter-of-fact way, as if to convey that you have something important on your mind. Make no small talk to get things started. If you have a secretary or assistant, say—in the employee's presence—something like, "Will you please hold my calls? I am going to have an important conversation and I don't want any interruptions."

Why so matter-of-fact? Because you want to make clear that you will have this conversation with the employee in your role as his boss. You want to set the stage in such a way as to leave him feeling just a little uncomfortable at the start of the meeting. Your goal is to get his attention. You apparently haven't up to now because he has not responded to your coaching as you had hoped. So you want to conduct this meeting on your terms and in a way that is most likely to be taken seriously by the person at the other end of the conversation.

STRUCTURING THE INTERVIEW

You will notice that the bottom right of the Formal Coaching Interview Form includes the outline of the structure for the interview. We are about to examine how to structure the interview and maintain control of the conversation. The following six steps are included on the Form to assist you in structuring the conversation.

1. *Ask the employee to listen to you first.*

Begin by saying something like, "I want to have a very important conversation with you, and I have prepared for this meeting by taking some notes. I know that you will have a point of view to share with me, and I certainly want to hear it. But first, I want to ask you to listen carefully and hear me out."

2. *Communicate your views.*

You will have in your hand the notes you organized on the Formal Coaching Interview Form. Using your notes as a guide, you will now communicate everything you have written, including what steps you will be forced to take next if the employee doesn't make the required changes.

As you will see in the sample interview below, you will not allow the employee to derail this conversation by interrupting you and taking the interview off track. You have prepared what you are going to say and you have a structure to follow. One of the reasons managers put off serious conversations about performance is that they allow themselves to be interrupted. Then the conversation spirals out of control and they never do get their message across.

3. *Ask for a restatement.*

Do you know the number one reason that people don't follow instructions from their doctor? Because they don't hear the instructions in the first place. For many people, going to a doctor is stressful and under stress, we don't listen very well. The same thing happens in this interview.

What is the employee most likely doing the entire time you are communicating what you have written? He is most likely preparing his defense. So you want to ask the employee to put into his own words what he heard you saying. What is the behavior that concerns you? What are your expectations of him from now on? If he leaves out important points or distorts what you have said, you then restate what you said until he understands you.

4. *Ask for the employee's views.*

Up to this point, this interview has been conducted entirely on your terms, and your approach has been very serious. Again, your tone has been serious, not angry or punitive in any way. Now you want to switch gears entirely. The sample interview presented below illustrates what you might say at this point to make clear that you are on the employee's side, that you know he doesn't want to fail, and that you just want to understand this situation as he sees it.

5. *Ask for a commitment.*

After exploring the situation from the employee's point of view, you will once again restate what you are asking him to do from now on. Don't settle for anything less than a commitment that he will meet your expectations from now on. Don't accept any form of "I'll try" or "I'll do my best."

6. *Promise follow-up.*

You want the employee to leave your office knowing that this conversation isn't over yet. You'll promise two kinds of follow-up: One, you will let him know that you'll be paying close attention and giving him additional coaching as needed. Two, you will ask him to get out his schedule before he leaves your office and set an appointment to review his progress in a month or six weeks from now.

THE IMPORTANCE OF FOLLOW-UP

You have just conducted a meeting to let someone know that you are running out of patience and that you want to see evidence of the changes you have been asking for. Now is the time to be looking for any evidence of movement in the right direction and to acknowledge it with praise. With complex behavioral changes, you may have to provide mixed coaching for a while, letting the employee know what you see in terms of improvement as well as how he needs to continue to improve.

Follow-up coaching helps lock in any movement in the right direction. It also lets the employee know that you are paying close attention to his performance, just as you promised you would in the interview. Knowing that you are paying attention is a factor in encouraging change.

Case Study: Sample Formal Coaching Interview

Kathleen, the CIO of a large financial services company, had recently been charged with studying the institution's IT systems and redesigning it to reduce costs and to make far more services available to their internal and external customers. Focus groups had revealed that private customers and the business community perceived the organization to be falling behind the rest of the industry in terms of the number of services provided and the convenience of getting those services.

The Challenge

Kathleen was hired because of her reputation for developing IT divisions that are on the leading edge, applying innovative technological solutions to create efficiencies in operations at lower costs while also offering innovative services to the organization's private and business customers

Kathleen carefully assembled a task force that included all the necessary technical disciplines to develop a comprehensive technological plan. One of the people she selected for the group is Elmer, a specialist in developing enhanced features for the company's IT systems. She picked Elmer because of his systems and network design skills. He is reputed to be not only the best in the company but is recognized as one of the best in the financial industry.

While Elmer is a brilliant professional, he has a reputation for arrogance and leaping to conclusions. In addition, his reputation within the organization was less than stellar. In previous projects, he irritated people in those projects by failing to listen and learn about their unique needs and methods of operations. He can be abrupt, difficult to persuade once he makes up his mind, and overly aggressive in discussions designed for problem identification and action planning. The irony of the situation is that Elmer turns out to be right almost every time. People end up happy with the outcome but extremely irritated by the process.

After selecting Elmer, she called him into her office and told him of her concerns about his relationship skills. This project is going to involve working with every function of the organizational internally. The task force is also going to be making a number of contacts with external customers, especially in segments of the business community that offer the greatest opportunities for increased business.

Elmer was going to have to change his ways, she told him. She had already heard from some internal customers that they felt Elmer was brilliant but that they didn't want to have to waste time dealing with his interpersonal quirks. They also expressed concerns that his behavior might alienate external customers to the extent that the organization might lose them, in spite of dramatically enhanced services

Kathleen knew that she had to start getting Elmer under control from the very beginning of the project. "Elmer, you are the best at what you do. That is why I chose you. But I have strong reservations about your relationship abilities. You have a reputation for being a 'know it all' who alienates people by leaping to conclusions and not being open to persuasion when people disagree with you. I've also been told that you come across as arrogant, but I am too new here to understand what people mean by that.

"I want you to know that I will be watching you closely and providing coaching to address any problems with relationships in this project. I need your skills. There is no one in the organization who can come close to matching your technological abilities. But I also need you to work effectively with the members of the task force and with the customers we'll be asking to participate in focus groups. So I just wanted to put you on notice that I'll be watching your performance carefully."

The Next Three Months.

True to his reputation, Elmer turned out to be a brilliant thinker, but one who alienated the very people whose cooperation and buy-in was required for a successful redesign of the systems that would produce new business as well as lower internal costs and produce increased efficiencies.

During the three months following her initial meeting with Elmer, Kathleen held several corrective coaching sessions with him. During one of the first sessions, she said to him: "Elmer, I want to talk to you about something I noticed in the meeting with the internal marketing group today. I'd been told you can come across as arrogant and I saw an example of that today. When Marie expressed doubt about new network features you want to design that will expand consumer services, it was clear to me that she didn't understand the technology behind the idea and that had created doubt in her mind about it working. You reacted by laughing. That's right. You actually laughed in her face. Then you explained the process to Marie in a tone of voice that sounded like you were talking to a five-year-old. You even said, 'I know this is difficult for someone like you to grasp but . . .' and then you went on to describe the process in an almost insulting level of simplicity.

"I noticed that Marie was embarrassed and left the meeting looking very upset. Marie has a lot of influence on opinions that get formed in her area. In fact her influence goes far beyond you'd think, given her title. You alienated an important person we need to have on our side. From now on, I want you to completely dispense with laughing at people who don't understand you immediately. It conveys disdain. In addition, I want you to paraphrase what people are saying to make sure you understand them. Finally, I don't want to hear that superior tone of voice from you ever again. I want you to speak with a friendly tone of voice and smile now and then."

On another occasion, Kathleen said to Elmer:

"I want to talk to you about the meeting we had with the business leaders today. This is difficult for me to describe but let me try. Your attitude in the meeting seemed to convey that these people run muffler shops, grocery stores, gas stations, and clothing stores and that they couldn't possibly understand what we were talking about. When people asked questions about how the technology would affect their business, I noticed that you would sigh, shake your head, and explain your answer again with an edge of irritation and impatience in your voice and on your face.

These people are our customers and we want to retain them as customers. The last thing I want any member of the task force doing is alienating people who are graciously donating their time to serve in a focus group to help us better understand their needs and discover new ways we can serve them.

"You need to control your irritation. Of course they don't understand the technology. That is not the business they are in. Stop acting so irritated when people ask for clarifications. It is only natural that they would want more information so that they can understand what we are offering them."

For several weeks, Kathleen continued to give Elmer corrective feedback but it just wasn't producing much change in Elmer's behavior. So she took the Coaching Preparation Worksheet to several meetings and started gathering observations in preparation for a Formal Coaching Interview. When she felt she had enough information, she organized it and transferred it to the Formal Coaching Interview Form.

She set up the meeting for the next day. As you read the sample interview, pay careful attention to what Kathleen says and how she uses the structure to maintain control of the meeting. You will also notice that at times she just ignores something Elmer says and goes right on with her written preparation. Also notice how she handles the change in the tone of the interview when she gets to the point of asking for Elmer's point of view.

[*Note*: For the sake of simplicity, I have dispensed with quotation marks. Anything written in italics describes nonverbal gestures or expressions.]

The Interview

Elmer arrives in Kathleen's office. Making no small talk, she asks him to take a seat across the desk from her, after which she phones her administrative assistant.

Kathleen: Scott, I am going to have a very important conversation with Elmer. I've put my calls on hold and I want to make sure that we are not interrupted during this meeting. So please stay at your desk until I'm finished and stop anyone from barging in on us.

Kathleen now looks serious, with an expression on her face that conveys she has something important to talk about with Elmer.

Kathleen: Elmer, I want to talk to you about your performance on the task force. I know that you will want to respond to what I am saying, and I do want to hear your point of view. But I have thought a lot about this meeting and have done some written preparation. I would like to ask you to sit quietly and hear me out first. Then I want to get your side of the issue. Is that okay with you?

Elmer: Okay.

Kathleen: Elmer, what I want to talk to you about is nothing new. We've been talking about your performance on the task force for some time now and about my concerns about your interactions with people both on the task force and with internal and external customers. For some time I've been concerned about how you treat people who don't know as much about the technology as you do. Your behavior includes laughing at people who ask you a question. The laugh is combined with an expression on your face that conveys that you think the other person is really dense.

At other times, your behavior is demeaning, especially with small business owners. When they ask basic questions about technology and how it might help them, you look put out, you sigh, and you get an irritated or bored look on your face. Then you answer the question in a tone of voice that suggests that even a third grader would already know the answer to this question.

Elmer: Look, I've been working real hard on . . .

Kathleen holds up her hand and leans forward.

Kathleen: I know you have a point of view and I want to hear it. But first I want you to listen. Now where was I? I have had some complaints from your coworkers that you have been difficult to work with.

Elmer: Who's been complaining?

Kathleen: That is not important and I want to again ask you not to interrupt me. Your coworkers tell me that when the group meets for brainstorming sessions, you very quickly make up your mind and, once you do, you stop listening . . .

Elmer: That's not true . . .

Kathleen: You stop listening and are no longer willing to look at a question or problem to find other ways to approach it. Here is the bottom line. You have a pattern of behaviors that make you very difficult to work with. You are impatient with people who don't know as much as you do. Your nonverbals include rolling your eyes, sighing loud enough to be heard by everyone at the table, shaking your head. You are also very difficult to persuade once you have made up your mind about something.

Your behavior is causing me some real concerns. I am getting to the point where I don't want to put you in front of a customer group for fear that you will insult them and actually lose customers who have been kind enough to give us their time for a focus group. I am also getting complaints from your coworkers, some of whom don't want you on the task force any longer.

Elmer: Who said that?

Kathleen: In addition, your behavior is not in keeping with our corporate values of treating each other and our customers with kindness, respect, and courtesy. Now, I have been asking you to make changes.

Elmer: Yeah, and I've really been working on them.

Kathleen: The changes I am asking for are not all that difficult. I want you to stop sighing, stop rolling your eyes, and I want you to stop acting like anyone who doesn't know something you know is an idiot. Instead, I'm asking you to smile and paraphrase questions when customer focus groups ask about something they don't know. And I expect you to keep smiling and convey verbally and nonverbally that you want nothing more than to answer their questions. Finally, I am asking you to be more open to input from the task force members and to stop reaching conclusions so fast. Once you reach a conclusion, the conversation is over for you and you stop listening or being open to looking at things from a different point of view.

Elmer: Come on, Kathleen. It isn't that bad. I've been . . .

Kathleen: Hold on. I'm just about finished. Here's where I stand on this issue right now. If your behavior doesn't change, I'm going to be forced to take you off the task force. I don't want to have to do that but I will unless you soften your approach to dealing with people.

There are two reasons I don't want to do this. First of all, you are the best person in the entire company in your specialty. I need your skills to make this project work at its best. Second, taking you off the task force is a black mark on your record. This is a high visibility project and everyone will know that you were booted off the team. Given your reputation for being hard to get along with, they'll reach their own conclusions why.

Elmer: Is it my turn to talk now?

Kathleen: Not quite. I've been giving you feedback and coaching you, but you haven't responded. It makes me wonder if you have understood me. So I want you to put into your own words what aspects of your performance have been of concern to me.

Elmer: You think I am a horrible person.

Kathleen: No, that is not what I said. I was much more specific than that. What behaviors have I been asking you to change?

Elmer: You want me to stop being so rude.

Kathleen: No, I've been more specific than that. What behaviors have been of concern to me?

Elmer: Well, you'd like me to stop rolling my eyes and stuff.

Kathleen: That's right. Rolling your eyes. What else have I asked you to change?

Elmer: You want me to stop treating customers in focus groups like idiots.

Kathleen: Close but I said something more specific. When people ask a simple question, you look very impatient, you sigh, and you answer questions in a tone of voice that conveys disdain. What do I want you to do differently around your coworkers on the task force?

Elmer: To roll over and play dead.

Kathleen: That is an exaggeration, Elmer, and you know it. You can do better than that.

Elmer: You want me to agree with them all the time?

Kathleen: No, in brainstorming sessions, I don't want you to make up your mind so quickly about the right answer. Instead, I want you to remain open to the possibility that continued discussions might come up with better solutions. When you stop listening, you stop contributing and it also has a dampening effect on the discussion.

Kathleen smiles and her tone of voice becomes much more friendly.

Kathleen: I've been giving you specific coaching on changes I want you to make and you haven't been making them. Help me understand that. I know you are a very intelligent man and I am not asking you to do anything you can't do. What is going on with you?

Elmer: I don't know. I've always been this way. No one has ever complained about it and I do keep getting promoted.

Kathleen: Of course you've been promoted. You are very good at what you do. Nevertheless, I find your behavior to be unacceptable. And I am willing to bet you've bothered people with this behavior whether or not they've said anything about it. Put yourself in their shoes. How would you feel if you asked a question and someone looked at you like they couldn't believe that you are so stupid that you don't already know the answer.

Elmer: I think I'd get pretty mad.

Kathleen: Of course you would. Can you see how these kinds of behaviors put people off?

Elmer: Yeah, I suppose.

Kathleen: Yet you keep doing them. Look. I believe in a basic law of human behavior. If a behavior persists, even though it may have negative consequences on our careers or our relationships, there must be a payoff somewhere.

Elmer: What do you mean by payoff?

Kathleen: I mean that you get something from behaving this way. What do you suppose you get out of acting this way around other people?

Elmer: I don't know.

Kathleen: Look harder. If these behaviors didn't pay off in some way, you wouldn't act that way. You would behave differently. But since you act that way, there must be a payoff somewhere. What do you get out of this?

Elmer: I can't think of anything.

Kathleen: How about feeling superior to those around you? Your behavior suggests that you know more than anyone else and that you feel a need to let them know that.

Elmer: Well, I *do* know more than a lot of other people know.

Kathleen: I know. That is why I put you on the task force. But if you rub peoples' noses in it, what is it costing you? In what ways is acting so superior going to damage your career?

Elmer: Well, I suppose people might start avoiding me.

Kathleen: I should think so. No one likes to work with someone who has to keep reminding people of their superior intellect. What do you gain out of coming to conclusions so quickly?

Elmer: Well, I am right most of the time. The answers are so obvious to me.

Kathleen: You're absolutely right. Almost every time you reach a conclusion in a short time, you are right. But when you shut down and stop participating, what impact does that have on those around you?

Elmer: I suppose they would get pretty irritated with me.

Kathleen: Yes. So irritated that several have already asked that you be removed from the task force.

Elmer: Who has been complaining?

Kathleen: You know I'm not going to tell you that. When people come to me with complaints, I start paying closer attention. We're having this conversation because I am concerned about your behavior, not because your teammates have complained.

I want you to know that this is not an idle conversation. Our guiding principles call on each and every one of us to treat each other and our customers with the utmost of respect. I cannot allow you to continue to openly violate those values. Our guiding principles are, in effect, promises we all agreed to keep. So I am expecting you to abide by them.

Elmer, I have asked you to make some specific changes in the past and you haven't made those changes. I am asking you to make a commitment. I've asked you to stop laughing at people, sighing and rolling your eyes. I've asked you to stop making faces and using a tone of voice that conveys the other person is stupid. I've asked you to remain more open to possibilities when brainstorming with your teammates. Can I count on you to do what I've asked from now on?

> Elmer: Well . . . I'll try.
>
> Kathleen: Elmer, trying isn't good enough. There is only doing or not doing. I know I'm not asking you to do something you can't do. I want to hear you say, "yes," that you'll do what I am asking of you.
>
> Elmer: Well, okay then. I'll do it. But this won't be easy for me.
>
> Kathleen: I will be paying close attention to you in the next few weeks. I'll be observing you and providing you with as much coaching support as I possibly can. You are a valuable member of this team. I need your technical skills and I'll do everything I can to help you develop a softer and kinder way of dealing with people.
>
> Did you bring your schedule? Good. Lets set an appointment for six weeks from now to review your progress. I'll be coaching you so much between then and now that I hope all I have to do in that meeting is talk about how much progress we've made.

FOLLOW-UP COACHING

You promised follow-up, and so you must deliver on that promise. You want the employee to know that you meant it when you said you'd be observing him closely for a while. For example, after the next task force meeting, Kathleen might call Elmer aside and say:

"I want to follow up on the conversation we had in my office the other day. During the team meeting, I noticed that when Alice disagreed with you, you made a real effort to control yourself. You did look a little irritated but you paraphrased her objection to see if you understood her correctly. Then you said something I thought was really effective. You responded by saying that you could see how the data would lead one to reach that conclusion but that if you factor in customer satisfaction, one might be led to reach an entirely different conclusion. You're moving in the right direction. Keep up working on it."

Difficult employees like Elmer can be turned around. It will take a great deal of patience on your part and continued observations with coaching to lock in appropriate behaviors while continuing to provide corrective coaching to work on needed improvements.

In reading the sample interview above, you might have asked yourself why anyone would put up with someone like Elmer. Remember that he is one of the best in his field. It is also highly probable that he grew up as a geek and an outcast. He never learned to interact with people because they didn't accept him. He probably responded by turning into an obnoxious know-it-all.

If Elmer's skills were anything less than stellar, you'd probably move him out of the organization. But with his technical abilities, you would be fully justified in doing everything you can to smooth some of the rough edges off his personality. Remember this: Emotional intelligence is open to change. With continuous observation, praise for even small movements in the right direction, and corrective coaching, people like Elmer can be brought around to a much more workable way of dealing with people.

No one wants to fail, even people like Elmer. Keep appealing to their innate desire to succeed and you'll be surprised at how much people can change.

THE FORMAL COACHING INTERVIEW FORM
(Personal and Confidential)

_____   _____

Employee   *Date of Conversation*

Coaching Format

I want to talk to you about *(describe the general topic).*

I've observed *(describe the pattern of behaviors and/or results).*

I am concerned about this because *(describe the impact of the problem).*

From now on, I'd like you to *(describe what you want the employee to do).*

If this situation continues, I will *(describe your next step).*

Summary (completed after the meeting)

Structuring the Interview
1. Ask employee to listen first.
2. Communicate your views.
3. Ask for a restatement.
4. Ask for employee's views.
5. Ask for a commitment.
6. Promise follow-up.

CHAPTER 13

THE LIMITATIONS OF COACHING

EARLY IN MY CAREER, I brought an enthusiastic optimism to executive coaching. I believed that everyone deserved a chance and that almost anyone could be coached and develop the skills necessary to succeed in a management or line position. All they needed was direct and specific feedback enabling them to see how others are seeing them and the unintended damage they were doing to themselves, to people with whom they worked, and their company and the customers their company served.

Given this information, they would see the light and respond positively to my coaching. And all would be well. If only it could be that simple.

It didn't take much experience as an executive coach to discover that I was investing my clients' time and money in coaching projects that were doomed to fail from the very start. I learned that not every manager or employee would make the dramatic changes I had promised. For a time, I struggled with accepting the fact that not everyone is a good candidate for coaching. But I soon realized that I had an obligation to deal with reality as it is, not as I wished it to be.

INVEST YOUR COACHING TIME WISELY

You have more than enough to do in your role as a manager or executive. Take some time to evaluate the people who report to you and make sure you are making the best use of your coaching time. Your employees will fall into one of these categories:

1. *The Outstanding Performer.* Make sure you let your best performers know how much you appreciate their contributions. A great performance appraisal is a good start but look for opportunities to acknowledge good performance. Additional responsibilities that give these employees the opportunity to develop new abilities and prepare them for promotion is another way of letting these people know they are valued and have a good future in your company.

2. *The Average Performer.* Most of your employees will fall into this category. These are the people who come to work every day and do what is expected of them. Every now and then, they may do something that is noteworthy. This will grab your attention and you may thank them for their efforts.

But most of the time, their performance is so dependable and reliable that you may not pay much attention to them. Even though their performance is adequate, you may be missing opportunities to offer coaching that will help them improve and develop greater mastery over the technical and interpersonal demands of their jobs.

In assessing each of your employees, you have to also take a good look at yourself. Are you devoting enough time to sharing your knowledge and experience and helping your employees continually develop their job skills and knowledge as well as their emotional intelligence? Truly great leaders never settle for "good enough." They are always looking for ways to inspire people to higher levels of performance by providing a combination of vision and coaching.

3. *The Employee Whose Performance Is Unacceptable but Who Is a Good Candidate for Coaching.* Inevitably, you will be faced with coaching someone who is failing to meet your expectations. She may

be failing to meet performance objectives or display unacceptable levels of emotional intelligence, such as treating customers or fellow employees rudely.

At the same time, she may be a good candidate for coaching. She might be new to the job and still developing the knowledge and skills necessary to perform well. She may have all the attributes you look for in an employee but need more coaching to master the abilities required for her to do her job well. With a mix of praise and corrective feedback, she will probably do quite well.

Someone else may have shortcomings in his emotional intelligence. For example, he may behave inappropriately in interactions with others on the job. But he has been responsive to corrective coaching in the past. He also strikes you as someone who means well but who is oblivious to his impact on people. Corrective coaching to raise his self-awareness and develop alternative ways of handling interactions more appropriately might be all it takes to smooth out some of the rough edges in his personality.

4. *The Marginal or Problem Employee.* If someone has failed to respond to coaching and continues to perform at a marginal or substandard level, start documenting the performance or behavioral problems as indicated by your company policies. You need to separate him from your company as soon as possible. You can't afford to let a marginal performer survive on your team. Everything you do as a leader sends a message. It is impossible to have a marginal employee on board without other people on the team noticing it. Sooner or later, such an employee will be cause for resentment as other people have to pick up the slack for the one who isn't pulling his weight.

MAKING THE CALL: WHEN TO COACH AND WHEN TO CUT BAIT

In making your assessments of managers and employees and their suitability for coaching, take a close and realistic look at the following factors:

1. How far off the mark are they?
2. Are they willing to take ownership of the change process?
3. Has too much damage already been done?
4. Do you have time to invest in this person?

How Far Off the Mark Are They?

Some people are so deficient in the development of emotional intelligence that coaching is likely to fail. The gap between where they are now and where they need to be may be too great for coaching to bring them around in a reasonable time. Coaching can produce remarkable changes in people. But someone's life experiences and values may have led to such serious deficiencies in their emotional intelligence that they can't help but do damage to the organization and the people in it. You have no choice but to move these people out of their positions. Confer with HR and start taking action to remove such people as soon as possible.

One of my clients, Chuck Cochrane, offered a way of thinking about the impact of people who are not capable of getting the job done. Suppose you have an organization of 1,000 employees. Those employees represent an average of three people per household. That means that your organization is responsible for feeding and clothing 3,000 people. If some people in the organization are not pulling their weight, you have no choice but to take action. You have 3,000 people depending on the success of the company to make sure their basic needs are taken care of.[3] As Jim Collins put it in his book, *Good To Great,* first you have to make sure you have the right people on board the bus.[4] Then you can take the bus anywhere you want to go.

Are They Willing to Take Ownership of the Change Process?

One of the assessments you have to make is whether or not the people you are coaching will take personal ownership of the problem and work hard to make the necessary changes. In talking with people, you must make clear that half-hearted cooperation with coaching is not going to get the job done. They need to see the coaching as an opportunity to save their jobs and that significant progress is expected. You should also establish milestones to be met in a short time, allowing you to take action quickly if change is not forthcoming.

I once encountered a manager who managed by fear and intimidation. He was "hardnosed and proud of it." He believed that people performed at their best when pushed to the limit and didn't see anything wrong with his management style. He was so locked into his beliefs that he was unwilling to acknowledge the damage he was doing to the organization and his people.

While you want to bring a level of compassion and understanding to coaching for emotional intelligence, don't waste time trying to remake a person's character and personality. In talking to people, trust your "gut reaction" when you think that coaching is going to be a waste of time. Some may make vague promises "to try" or "do my best" but if you think she is only saying what she thinks you want to hear so you'll get off her back, you are probably right. When someone is committed to make a change, you will know it from what she says and how she says it. If an employee is only half-heartedly willing to change, don't waste your time.

Has Too Much Damage Already Been Done?

Sometimes you will encounter employees who have done so much damage to their reputations and their relationships with their co-workers that their credibility is beyond repair, no matter how hard they might try to change.

I once worked with a president of one of my clients' wholly-owned subsidiaries. She was technically skilled but so unsure of herself that she took far too long to make decisions and would often change them later. Her indecisiveness and constantly changing goals had badly damaged her team's ability to get the job done.

By the time I met her, she had lost all professional credibility with her staff. They had started referring to her as a "Barbie doll with a briefcase." Even if coaching could have taught her to walk on water, her people would probably just end up complaining that "Barbie can't swim."

You may occasionally run into people like this when you take over a new team as a result of a transfer or promotion. Leaving a lost cause in position can only end in damaging your credibility. Letting such people go quickly sends the message that you are serious about setting high standards for performance and the ability of people to work effectively with other team members.

Do You Have Time to Invest in This Person?

You may one day find yourself in the position of being brought in to lead a team that is not coping well with a change that is essential for the success of the organization. Your own boss is expecting you to turn the team around and to do it quickly.

In these cases, you must do assessments of your people's technical and organizational skills. Sometimes you'll find long-term employees whose technical skills were sufficient to take the company to a certain level of success but now those same skills are not enough to take the company where it needs to go. Or you may find that some people on the team are resisting change and creating problems for others on the team who are embracing new directions. In such cases, you have no choice but to let them go and find people who are more suitable for the job.

A FAILURE OF NERVE

I have been involved in a number of terminations over the course of my career. I have never been involved in a termination that was too early. Almost always, the termination was long overdue. And in most cases, the upper management knew all along that they should be taking this action but hadn't done it until an outsider came in and prodded them to do what they know they should have done long ago.

I find this to be very troubling, especially when it involves people in management positions. Incompetent managers do great damage to their organizations. Sometimes they get away with it because their technical skills are badly needed. Other times, they just get away with it simply because senior management hasn't had the courage to take action.

These managers have a great deal to do with the quality of lives of the people in their organizations. Middle managers and first-line managers establish an environment that people live and work in forty or more hours every week. Bad managers create pockets within the organization that is so toxic to the people in it that work becomes a soul killer, draining all the life and vitality that is available to people who want only to do a good job and be treated with respect and appreciation.

If your work life doesn't work, it affects your entire life. I've met people who spend their entire careers on hold. Waiting for quitting time. Waiting for the weekend. Then lying in bed on Sunday night with dread of going back to work for yet another week. It is hard to live that way and be a happy person, a caring spouse, or a good friend.

Your courage and willingness to take action creates a ripple effect that can extend far beyond the workplace. Removing someone who is a toxic influence on the team will improve the quality of work the group accomplishes. And it will also improve the quality of their lives. If you need to let someone go, don't hesitate. Most of the time, you'll find that it results in a boost to the morale of coworkers who have been putting up with someone who hasn't been pulling his weight.

RESPONDING TO PSYCHOLOGICAL AND
PHYSICAL CONDITIONS

Coaching is not the answer to every performance problem. As a leader, you will occasionally encounter employees with psychological or physical conditions that are interfering with their ability to perform. This puts you in an awkward position. On the one hand, you are responsible to see to it that all employees who report to you do what is expected of them.

But if a physical or psychological condition is playing a role in the employee's failure to perform adequately, coaching will not resolve the problem.

To make matters even more complicated, if a physical or psychological problem is a factor, you may be limited in your ability to discipline or terminate an employee, no matter how poorly he might be performing. State and federal regulations may mandate that treatment, not discipline or termination, is your only recourse.

Psychological Disorders Encountered in the Workplace

First, a disclaimer. This section is not intended to make you capable of diagnosing any form of psychiatric disorder. Leave that to professionals trained to do this kind of work. My intention is to alert you to signs that indicate a psychiatric problem *may* account for an employee's inability to meet your expectations. If so, you have a moral, and perhaps even a legal, responsibility to encourage the employee to seek out a professional evaluation. Many companies offer Employee Assistance Programs designed for this very purpose.

The following list of psychological conditions is incomplete but these are the most common:

Clinical Depression

This condition can sometimes be seen as a profound change in mood that may seem to have no external cause. You might notice a radical change in productivity. The employee's sense of humor disappears. He may become socially withdrawn and no longer finding enjoyment in any aspect of his work. This condition can become so severe that people start calling in sick with some frequency and the person you used to know seems to be hidden under a cloud. We all have days when we might be feeling depressed for some reason. For most of us, these days come and go. If you have an employee who seems to be depressed for several weeks and his performance has noticeably deteriorated, a psychiatric evaluation may be indicated.

Clinical depression is mystifying in that it can strike people you would think would have everything going for them. They are often bright, successful people with a supportive family. Nevertheless, clinical depression can strike anyone, regardless of his external circumstances. Mike Wallace, of the television news program *60 Minutes*, has spoken eloquently of his long struggle with depression. He had success, fame, wealth, and work he loves to do but became so severely depressed that his life was sheer torment until he got the proper medication.

The problem with clinical depression is that someone may be too depressed to have the energy required to do anything about it. Under these conditions, your encouragement and support in seeking out an evaluation may literally save the person's life.

Reactive Depression

This is a less serious depressive episode triggered by life events. A death or an illness in the family, a divorce, or financial problems can lead to depression. This form of depression is responsive to a short course of psychotherapy that is sometimes supplemented with medication.

Chronic Anxiety

In some people, chronic and pervasive anxiety makes it difficult for them to function on the job. These are people who are so worried about so many things that it is difficult for them to maintain their attention on work. If asked, some will acknowledge that they are constantly anxious and worried, sometimes for reasons they themselves can't explain. They also tend to have frequent headaches and an exaggerated startle response. Anti-anxiety medication and psychotherapy can help someone afflicted with anxiety be a happier and more productive employee.

Attention Deficit Disorder in Adults

It was long thought that children with ADD grew out of it as adults. We now know that ADD and ADHD are far more prevalent in adults than we had previously thought. These people have trouble concentrating and completing tasks on time. They have difficulty getting started on large tasks that will take a great deal of organization. They might present the picture of a whirlwind of activity but not be accomplishing very much. They know what they need to do and they know how to do it, but for reasons that mystify even themselves, they just have trouble getting things done. They may be highly creative but their lack of organization makes it difficult for them to follow through with action.

Their thinking and behavior is marked by a short attention span and a high degree of disorganization. They might be highly impulsive in social interactions, interrupting frequently, often as not with topics that are off task. They may have trouble sitting still in meetings and fidget constantly.

The right medication can produce dramatic and life-changing differences in those who have remained undiagnosed and untreated into their adulthood. The response to the medication is so rapid that, if properly diagnosed and medicated, you will watch this person transform before your very eyes.

Alcohol and Drug Abuse

As much as you might like to think this can't happen on your watch, 7.5 percent of Americans employed full time report heavy drinking.

This is defined as having five or more drinks per day on five or more days in the past thirty days.[5] Problems with drinking or drug abuse on the job or shortly before work is costly, resulting in $81.6 billion in lost productivity due to premature death ($37 billion) and illness $44.6 billion.[6] Absenteeism among alcoholics and problem drinkers is 3.8 to 8.3 times greater than it is for the average employee. And up to 40 percent of industrial fatalities and 47 percent of industrial injuries can be linked to the consumption of alcohol.[7]

Of all the psychiatric disorders, alcoholism is one of the most difficult to deal with. Your inclination may be just to fire someone you suspect of coming to work with a hangover or smelling of alcohol. But firing an alcoholic without first attempting to get her into treatment puts your company at risk for a lawsuit under the Americans with Disabilities Act.

Physical Diseases

Sometimes a physical disorder can lead to a diminished capacity to produce results at work. If someone's performance and pace of work declines suddenly, you might not have a problem employee—you might have a sick employee.

I learned this lesson early in my career. I had given the EQ Profile to a senior executive in a large company. His energy score was extremely low, as were his optimism, work, and detail scores. The overall pattern of scores predicted that this person was doomed to fail in his position, particularly since the company had recently acquired another company. As controller of the company, his workload was going to be extremely high for the next few months and I had severe doubts about his ability to handle the pace and amount of work required.

It turned out that I was right but for the wrong reasons. I met with him to express my concerns and learned that he had been feeling terrible for the last six months. His energy level had fallen dramatically. He was barely able to drag himself out of bed to go to work. At night, he would come home exhausted and immediately go to bed. As men are prone to do, he had avoided seeing a doctor but his wife insisted he get a physical.

He had just been diagnosed with diabetes and was in the early stages of getting his illness under control with insulin, proper diet, and exercise. I called the CEO a few months later and was told that the controller had returned to his usual high level of performance.

MAKING A REFERRAL FOR AN EVALUATION

Never recommend a psychological or physical evaluation without first consulting with Human Resources. You will discover what is available to help the employee and how your organization's policies and legal requirements affect how you handle this situation.

If you have done a good job of building a relationship of trust with your employees, talking with the employee about your concerns will be much easier for both of you. Structure the conversation in much the same way you would structure coaching. Prepare for the conversation by gathering your observations of the employee, especially with reference to noticeable changes in his mood and performance.

Talk to the employee after reminding yourself that you want to handle this conversation with caring and concern. Her performance may have deteriorated to the point that you are frustrated but this is not the time for a corrective or disciplinary approach to the problem.

You might start the conversation like this: "Diana, I have become very concerned about you lately. You just haven't seemed like the same person I've come to know and depend on for such a long time. I've noticed a dramatic change in your mood. You used to have a pretty good sense of humor and to be happy with your work. But now you appear to be depressed, like a dark cloud is hanging over you. You rarely laugh. You don't contribute as much in team meetings as you used to. It is almost as if you are withdrawing into yourself.

"I've also noticed a worrisome decline in both the volume and speed of your work. I've even received some comments from some of your employees that they are concerned about you.

"While I'm concerned about the decline in your performance, I am much more concerned about what might be causing the problem. I am worried that you might be seriously depressed or that you might have some physical condition that is affecting your energy.

"Diana, help me understand what is going on with you. I want to know what I can do to help."

This conversation may go one of three directions:

1.   *The employee may open up to you.* She may admit to feelings of depression, perhaps because of problems at home. Or she may acknowledge that she hasn't been feeling well lately. If she opens up to you, you will already have talked with HR before the meeting and you'll be prepared to refer her to the correct resource to get an evaluation.

2.   *The employee may feel uncomfortable talking with you about it.* In this case, ask if she would be willing to speak with the resource you have lined up in HR. It is only natural that someone who is having personal problems may not feel comfortable talking about it with the boss.

3.   *The employee may deny there is any problem at all.* If you are dealing with an alcohol or drug problem, the employee will almost certainly deny it. Your contact with HR ahead of this meeting will tell you what your options are. For example, the company may be able to require a drug and alcohol screening test.

On the other hand, you may find that you have few viable options, given your state laws, union agreements, or company policies (or deficiencies thereof). In that case, you need to start building a case, documenting problems in performance, such as coming to work late, missed deadlines, poor relationships with coworkers or customers, etc. You can't fire someone for being an alcoholic. But you can fire someone with documented performance problems and the implementation of progressive discipline as mandated by company policies.

Reflections

1. Evaluate the people who report to you. Are you coaching people who are not making the necessary changes? In your heart, do you know that you need to stop hoping for a dramatic change and take steps to move one or more people out of their positions or out of the organization? If so, what is it costing you not to be taking action? What is it costing the people in that part of the organization? Why have you not acted up to now? Can you continue to live with yourself, knowing the impact this is having on the organization and the people who work for you?

2. Do you have someone on your team who might be in need of medical or psychiatric evaluation? If so, contact HR and find out what steps you can take to get this person the necessary attention.

NOTES

1. Chuck Cochrane is the president and CEO of Blethen Maine Newspapers, a subsidiary of the *Seattle Times*. He granted permission for me to share his metaphor for management.

2. Jim Collins, *Good to Great: Why Some Companies Make the Leap . . . and Others Don't* (New York: HarperCollins, 2001).

3. National Institute of Drug Abuse, *National Household Survey on Drug Abuse: Main Findings, 1994* (September 1996), p. 100.

4. U.S. Department of Health and Human Services, *Substance Abuse and Mental Health Statistics Sourcebook, 1990* (May 1995), p. 3.

5. National Institute of Drug Abuse, *National Household Survey.*

6. U.S. Department of Health and Human Services, *Substance Abuse Sourcebook.*

7. M. Bernstein and & J.J. Mahoney, "Management Perspectives on Alcoholism: The Employer's Stake in Alcoholism Treatment," *Occupational Medicine* 4, 2 (1989): 223–232.

AFTERWORD

WHEN YOU LEAD PEOPLE, it is like looking in a mirror. If you want to know how well you are doing as a leader, all you have to do is look at your team. They reflect your passion, commitment, clarity of purpose, and drive to produce results.

Leaders sometimes tell me how lucky they are. They go on to describe people who require just a little direction. Then all they have to do is get out of their team's way and the work gets done. There is no such thing as luck when it comes to producing good teamwork. You know that from your own experience. We have all seen a team that was once highly productive and upbeat that took a nosedive when someone else was brought in to manage the group.

The only useful assumption to make about leadership is that you are the source of everything you see in your team, day in and day out. Most of the time, what you see is good news. You are already doing a lot of things right. Otherwise, their performance would not be maintained at a high level for very long.

When people are not meeting your expectations, the only useful question to ask is, "How am I the source of this? What am I doing—or failing to do—that has them coming to work and failing to meet my standards? Have I been coaching them effectively? Have I been avoiding a conversation because it might get uncomfortable?

Did I attempt to coach without properly preparing and failing to get my message across?"

Coaching goes to the very heart of leadership. If you aren't coaching, you are not leading. The people you lead want nothing more than the gift of your appreciation for what they do and support in becoming the best that they can be. I've done my best to provide you with the tools. The rest is up to you.

With my best wishes, Bob.

RECOMMENDED READINGS

Albrecht, Karl. *Social Intelligence: The New Science of Success.* San Francisco: Jossey-Bass, 2006.

Bell, Chip. *Manager as Mentor, 2nd Edition.* San Francisco, Berrett-Koehler Publishers, 2002.

—— *Customer Love.* Executive Excellence, 2000.

Blanchard, Ken, and Michael O'Connor. *Managing By Values.* San Francisco, Berrett-Koehler Publishers, 1997.

Block, Peter. *Stewardship: Choosing Service Over Self-Interest.* San Francisco: Berrett-Keohler, 1993.

Buckingham, Marcus, and C. Coffman. *First, Break All the Rules: What the World's Greatest Managers Do Differently.* New York: Simon & Schuster, 1999.

Canfield, Jack, and Jacqueline Miller. *Heart at Work Stories and Strategies for Building Self-Esteem and Reawakening the Soul at Work.* New York: McGraw-Hill, 1996.

Chermiss, Cary, and Mitchel Adler. *Promoting Emotional Intelligence in Organizations.* Alexandria, Va.: American Society for Training and Development, 2000.

Collins, Jim. *Good To Great: Why Some Companies Make the Leap . . . and Others Don't.* New York: HarperCollins, 2001.

Conger, Jay A. *The Charismatic Leader.* San Francisco: Jossey-Bass Publishers, 1992.

Cooper, Robert K., and Ayman Sawaf. *Executive EQ Emotional Intelligence in Leadership and Organizations.* New York: The Berkley Publishing Group, 1997.

Covey, Stephen. *Principle-Centered Leadership.* New York: Summit Books, 1990.

—— *Working with Emotional Intelligence.* New York: Bantam Doubleday Dell, 2000.

DePree, Max. *Leadership Is an Art.* New York: Doubleday, 1998.

Fisher, Helen. *The First Sex: The Natural Talents of Women and How They Are Changing the World.* New York: Ballantine, 1999.

Goleman, Daniel. *Emotional Intelligence: Why It Can Matter More Than IQ.* New York: Bantam Books, 1995.

Goleman, Daniel, Boyatzis, Richard, and Annie McKee. *Primal Leadership.* Boston: Harvard Business School Press, 2002.

——. *Working with Emotional Intelligence.* New York: Bantam Books, 1998.

——, R. Boyatizis, and A. McKee. *Primal Leadership: Learning to Lead with Emotional Intelligence.* Boston: Harvard Business School Press, 2002.

Harmon, Frederick G. *Playing for Keeps.* New York: John Wiley & Sons Inc., 1996.

Hawley, Jack. *Reawakening the Spirit in Work.* New York: Simon & Schuster, 1993.

Herman, Stanley M. *The Tao at Work.* San Francisco: Jossey-Bass Publishers, 1994.

Jones, Laurie Beth. *Jesus CEO.* New York: Hyperion, 1995.

Kaye, Les. *Zen at Work.* New York: Crown Trade Paperbacks, 1996.

Kelley, Robert E. *How to be a Star at Work.* New York: Times Business, Random House, 1998.

Kouzes, James, and Barry Posner. *The Leadership Challenge.* San Francisco: Jossey-Bass Publishers, 1987.

Lencioni, Patrick. *The Five Dysfunctions of a Team: A Leadership Fable.* San Francisco: Jossey-Bass, 2002.

——. *Overcoming the Five Dysfunctions of a Team: A Field Guide for*

Leaders, Managers, and Facilitators. San Francisco: Jossey-Bass, 2005.

Lynn, Adele B. *The Emotional Intelligence Activity Book: 50 Activities for Developing EQ at Work.* New York: AMACOM, 2003.

———. *The EQ Difference: A Powerful Plan for Putting Emotional Intelligence to Work.* New York: AMACOM, 2005.

———. *In Search of Honor—Lessons From Workers on How to Build Trust.* Belle Vernon, Penn.: BajonHouse Publishing, 1998.

Salovey, Peter, PhD., and John Mayer, PhD. *Emotional Development and Emotional Intelligence.* New York: Basic Books, 1997.

Sanders, Tim. *The Likeability Factor: How to Boost Your L-Factor & Achieve Your Life's Dreams.* New York: Crown, 2005.

Sashkin, Marshall. *Becoming a Visionary Leader.* King of Prussia, Penn.: Organization Design and Development, 1986.

Simmons, Steve, and J.C. Simmons. *Measuring Emotional Intelligence: The Groundbreaking Guide to Applying the Principles of Emotional Intelligence.* Arlington, Tex.: Summit, 1997.

Sterrett, Emily. *The Managers Pocket Guide to Emotional Intelligence.* Amherst, Mass.: HRD Press, 2000.

Wall, Bob. *Working Relationships: The Simple Truth About Getting Along with Friends and Foes at Work.* Palo Alto, Calif.: Davies-Black Publishing, 1999.

———. *The Handbook of Interpersonal Skills Training: 16 Complete Training Modules for Building Working Relationships.* New York: McGraw-Hill, 2001.

Weisinger, Hendrie, PhD. *Emotional Intelligence at Work.* San Francisco: Jossey-Bass, 1997.

INDEX

ABOUT THE AUTHOR

BOB WALL, president of Wall Consulting, has been an independent consultant since 1980. He specializes in accelerating leadership, team, and cultural development. He provides in-depth assessments of individuals and teams. His services include executive coaching, team development, and tailoring training events and speaking services to meet the unique needs of his clients. He is the coauthor of *The Mission-Driven Organization*, and the author of *Working Relationships* and *The Handbook of Interpersonal Skills Training*. To learn more about Bob and the services he provides, visit his website at bobwallonline.com. He is now located in Connecticut after working out of the Seattle area for twenty years.